KRIK

Edwidge Danticat

AUTHORED by Amber Stewart
UPDATED AND REVISED by Aaron Suduiko

COVER DESIGN by Table XI Partners LLC
COVER PHOTO by Olivia Verma and © 2005 GradeSaver, LLC

BOOK DESIGN by Table XI Partners LLC

Published by GradeSaver LLC, www.gradesaver.com

First published in the United States of America by GradeSaver LLC. 2016

ISBN 978-1-60259-951-2

Printed in the United States of America

For other products and additional information please visit http://www.gradesaver.com

Table of Contents

Biography of Edwidge Danticat (1969–)

Edwidge Danticat is a Haitian-American novelist and short story writer born in Port-au-Prince, Haiti on January 19, 1969. When she was 2 years old, her parents fled Haiti because of the oppressive political regime of François Duvalier, a dictator who was president of Haiti for 14 years. Danticat and her younger brother André were unable to escape with their parents and were raised by their aunt and uncle. Thus, from an early age, Danticat was made aware of how Haiti's tumultuous political situation can impact personal narratives.

Eventually, Danticat and her brother were able to join their parents in Brooklyn when she was 12. They lived in a Haitian-American neighborhood where Danticat felt acutely her identity as an immigrant teenager. To cope with her disorientation, Danticat turned to literature. She had already begun writing in Haiti at age 9, using French and Haitian Creole to pen her stories. When she was 14 she published her first English story, "A Haitian-American Christmas: Cremace and Creole Theatre", in a citywide magazine written by teenagers. Following this first release, Danticat wrote another story about her immigration experience titled "A New World Full of Strangers." She recalls that after writing this story she felt that her personal narrative was unfinished. This feeling of incompleteness was in part the motivation for *Breathe, Eyes, Memory,* her first novel.

Danticat enrolled at Barnard College in New York City, intent on studying medicine at the behest of her parents. Her love of literature won out, however, and she graduated with a degree in French Literature. She went on to earn a MFA from Brown University in 1993. Her thesis for the Master's degree, titled "My turn in the fire—an abridged novel," was published as *Breathe, Eyes, Memory* in 1994, to critical acclaim. Four years after publication, it was selected as an Oprah's Book Club pick. Chronicling a girl's journey from Haiti to the U.S., *Breathe, Eyes, Memory* is in part autobiographical and showcases many of the recurring themes of Danticat's work, including diasporic politics, mother-daughter relationships, and gender-race identity.

Since *Breathe, Eyes, Memory* Danticat has continued to be a prolific writer in addition to teaching creative writing at New York University and Miami University. Writing both fiction and nonfiction, she still highlights the lives of Haitian people, focusing on political and societal injustice as well as interpersonal conflicts. *Krik? Krak!,* a collection of 10 short stories about women in Haiti, is one such work. Another notable work is *Brother, I'm Dying,* a memoir about the uncle who raised Danticat and her brother when they lived in Haiti. She also has a few non-prose projects, including collaborations with filmmakers Patricia Benoit and Jonathan Demme on documentaries about Haiti. In 2009, she narrated *Poto Mitan: Haitian Women Pillars of the Global Economy*, a documentary about five women from different generations and the role of globalization in their lives.

Danticat's work has received numerous awards and accolades, including the American Book Award, the National Book Critics Circle Award, and the Langston Hughes Medal. She also holds honorary degrees from Smith College and Yale University. Perhaps most impressively, American author Paule Marshall has praised Danticat for giving "a silenced Haiti…its literary voice" back. Today, Danticat lives with her husband and two daughters in Miami.

Krik? Krak! Study Guide

Published in 1995, *Krik? Krak!* is a collection of 9 short stories written by Haitian-American author Edwidge Danticat. Though they have differing topics and central characters, the stories are linked together because of one central concept: the relationships Haitian women have to their families and their country. The stories are set in Port au Prince, the fictional town of Ville Rose, and New York City over a span of years. The title of the collection, *Krik? Krak!,* is a Haitian phrase used to introduce a period of storytelling. The storyteller asks their audience "Krik?" and they reply "Krak!" Typically, the stories told during a Krik? Krak! session are lighthearted tales, jokes, riddles, etc. Therefore, Danticat's collection, which features stories of poverty, loss, death, struggle, and survival instead of humorous interludes, is a bit misleading.

Danticat has been praised for giving a silenced Haiti its voice back after the oppressive regimes of François Duvalier and his son Jean-Claude Duvalier. *Krik? Krak!* is one of the main texts Danticat wrote about the lives of pedestrian Haitians trying to survive under the Duvalier dictatorships. Danticat's own parents fled Haiti because of the Duvaliers, and Danticat herself lived for 12 years under Jean-Claude's dictatorship. This gives Danticat a unique personal connection to the stories she weaves in the collection. Few authors have tackled this history from this perspective or in the prose medium; that is the historical value of *Krik? Krak!*

In 1995, *Krik? Krak!* was nominated for the National Book Award for Fiction. Numerous critics and reviewers have praised the collection, calling it "virtually flawless" and "harsh, passionate, lyrical" (Washington Post Book World and The Seattle Times, respectively). The enduring power and popularity of *Krik? Krak!* lies in Danticat's ability to tell the stories that bring to life the history, hopes, and human experience of Haitian people.

Krik? Krak! Summary

"Children of the Sea"

"Children of the Sea" is the story of two star-crossed Haitian lovers separated by political persecution and disapproving parents. In a series of letters, the two characters write about life aboard a refugee boat and life under the oppressive Duvalier regime. Because it is not possible for the characters to actually exchange letters, the missives read more like diary entries than exchanges between two people. Still, their love for one another shines through, despite the distance that the sea (and eventually, death) creates between them.

"Nineteen Thirty-Seven"

Josephine and her mother Défilé move to Port-au-Prince in search of a better life, but soon after arriving Défilé's friend accuses her of being a witch. Défilé is arrested and sentenced to life in prison. Josephine is now alone, aside from a Madonna doll she inherited from her mother. She visits her mother frequently at the prison but never speaks to her. In flashbacks it is revealed that Défilé's mother was a victim of the 1937 massacre, and Défilé had to leap across the Massacre River to save herself and an unborn Josephine. At the end of the story Défilé dies because of the poor living conditions in the prison, but Josephine is at peace, knowing that her mother's final flight was joyful.

"A Wall of Fire Rising"

Guy, Lili, and Little Guy live in a shantytown in Haiti's countryside. Lili and Little Guy seem content with their lives, but Guy dreams of a life free from poverty. When a wealthy family in their town brings a hot air balloon there from America, Guy becomes obsessed with it. Nothing can curb his fascination–neither his wife's worry nor his son's triumphs at school. In the end, Guy is overcome by his obsession with the balloon and commits suicide after successfully flying it.

"Night Women"

"Night Women" is a night in the life of a Haitian sex worker. As she waits for one of her weekly patrons, the unnamed woman gazes upon her son and allows her mind to drift across a myriad of topics. Her most pressing thought concerns how she will continue to keep her sex work a secret from her child. Before long, her patron arrives and they conduct their business, undetected by her son. When her patron leaves, the woman goes outside to smoke a cigarette, reenters her house, and discovers her son has woken up. The story ends with her rocking her son back to sleep.

"Between the Pool and the Gardenias"

Marie, a young Haitian woman working as a maid for a bourgeois Haitian couple, finds an abandoned baby in the streets of Port-au-Prince. Ravaged by a slew of miscarriages, Marie thinks the baby is a gift from God and takes it home. Unfortunately for Marie, the baby is already dead and its body begins to decompose. She tries to give the baby a proper burial, but another employee of the wealthy couple discovers her. He reports her to the police, and the story ends with the pair of them waiting for the police to arrive.

"The Missing Peace"

Lamort is a 14-year-old girl living with her grandmother in Ville Rose. She is friends with a macoute named Raymond, and helps her grandmother run a small guesthouse. One day a foreigner looking for her journalist mother comes to stay at the guesthouse. Lamort agrees to help her, but during their search they run afoul of Raymond's friend Toto. Raymond helps rescue them, but his and Lamort's relationship is unequivocally changed. Despite this, the story ends on a somewhat positive note, with Lamort asking to be called Marie Magdalène, after her dead mother.

"Seeing Things Simply"

Princesse is a young girl that works as a model for a Guadeloupian painter named Catherine. On her way to Catherine's house Princesse passes by cockfights and a drunken old man. During her sessions with Catherine, Princesse discusses a range of topics, including art and the universe. One day Catherine disappears, and Princesse realizes that she also wants to paint the world around her. When Catherine returns, she gives Princesse one of the portraits she modeled for. The gift inspires Princesse to make her first drawing, a dirt drawing of the drunken old man and his wife.

"New York Day Women"

Suzette is a Haitian immigrant living in New York City with her parents. Her mother in particular finds many aspects of life in America difficult to assimilate to. Thus, Suzette is shocked when she sees her mother strutting in Manhattan as if she owns the streets. Her interest piqued, Suzette follows her mother as she moves through the city. She watches as her mother babysits a young boy and meets up with some other immigrant women. The story ends with Suzette rushing back to her office, her perspective on her mother thoroughly shaken.

"Caroline's Wedding"

Grace, Caroline, and their mother Hermine are a Haitian family living in New York City. Grace, Hermine, and the deceased father/husband were born in Haiti, while Caroline was born in America. To Hermine's chagrin, Caroline is marrying Eric, a Bahamian man with a speech impediment. Though Grace doesn't vocalize it, she also has reservations about Caroline's upcoming marriage, because she feels as if her sister is abandoning the family. By the story's denouement, Caroline and Eric do get married, and Hermine and Grace learn that Caroline's wedding isn't an ending, but a beginning.

Epilogue: "Women Like Us"

"Women Like Us" is *Krik? Krak!'s* epilogue. It tells the story of a young woman who attracts the ire of her mother when she confesses that she wants to be a writer. Despite her mother's anger, the young woman tells the stories of her female ancestors.

Krik? Krak! Characters

The male letter writer

One of the protagonists of "Children of the Sea." After the military raids his radio show, he attempts to flee to the United States for political immunity.

The female letter writer

The other protagonist of "Children of the Sea." She and the male letter writer are in love, but her father does not approve of the relationship. She remains in Haiti with her parents and hides from the military in the provinces.

Papa

The father of the female protagonist in "Children of the Sea." He is practical and focuses on keeping his family safe, which means he often ignores the injustices happening around him.

Manman

The mother of the female protagonist in "Children of the Sea."

Célianne

In "Children of the Sea," she is a young pregnant woman also trying to escape to the United States via boat. In "Caroline's Wedding," a mass is held for her at Saint Agnes Church in New York City.

Madan Roger

In "Children of the Sea," she is the mother of a young revolutionary who was killed for his controversial beliefs.

Uncle Pressoir

The uncle of the female protagonist in "Children of the Sea."

Josephine

The protagonist of "Nineteen Thirty-Seven." She lives alone now because her mother was imprisoned for allegedly performing witchcraft.

Madonna

Josephine's doll, passed down from her great-great-great-grandmother.

Manman/Défilé

In "Nineteen Thirty-Seven," she is Josephine's mother. Défilé is also the name of Josephine's great-great-great-grandmother.

El Generalissimo

In "Nineteen Thirty-Seven," he is the Dominican general in charge of the massacre of many Haitians living in the Dominican Republic.

Jacqueline

In "Nineteen Thirty-Seven," she is an old woman who comes to tell Josephine about her mother's life in prison.

Guy

The male protagonist of "A Wall of Fire Rising," he is married to Lili and is the father of Little Guy. He is obsessed with a hot air balloon owned by the Assad family.

Lili

In "A Wall of Fire Rising," she is the wife of Guy and the mother of Little Guy. Nurturing and caring, she worries about her husband's obsession with the hot air balloon. In "Between the Pool and the Gardenias," we learn that Lili commits suicide in her older years.

Little Guy

In "A Wall of Fire Rising," he is the son of Guy and Lili. The title of the short story is derived from a play Little Guy performs at school about a slave revolution.

The Assads

In "A Wall of Fire Rising," a Haitian family of Lebanese or Palestinian descent that owns a sugar mill and the hot air balloon with which Guy is obsessed.

The Night Woman

In "Night Women," she is the unnamed protagonist who struggles with keeping her nighttime suitors a secret from her young son.

The Night Woman's Son

In "Night Women," he is the son of the night woman and is seemingly unaware of how his mother provides their livelihood.

Emmanuel

In "Night Women," he is one of the night woman's suitors. He is a doctor and visits on Tuesdays and Saturdays.

Alexandre

In "Night Women," he is one of the night woman's suitors. He is an accordion player and visits on Mondays and Thursdays.

Marie

The protagonist of "Between the Pool and the Gardenias," she has had many miscarriages. Her grief over her lost children causes her to hallucinate and think that Rose is still alive.

Rose

In "Between the Pool and the Gardenias," she is a child who was abandoned by her parents in the streets of Haiti. She is dead, but Marie thinks she is alive and takes her home.

Madame

Marie's employer in "Between the Pool and the Gardenias." Marie steals Madame's perfume to mask the smell of Rose's decomposition.

Monsieur

Marie's employer in "Between the Pool and the Gardenias."

The Dominican

In "Between the Pool and the Gardenias," he is a Dominican man who also works for Madame and Monsieur. He and Marie had sex once.

Lamort

The protagonist of "The Missing Peace," she lives with her grandmother because her mother died during childbirth. For this reason she is named "Lamort," which means "the death."

Lamort's grandmother

In "The Missing Peace," she is the grandmother of "Lamort." Strict with her granddaughter, she manages to provide a good life for the pair of them by renting rooms.

Marie Magdaléne

In "The Missing Peace," she is the dead mother of Lamort.

Raymond

In "The Missing Peace," he is a soldier in the new regime. He is friends with Lamort and tries unsuccessfully to seduce her.

Toto

In "The Missing Peace," he is a solider in the new regime. He once shot Raymond in the leg because he did not know if he was part of the old or new regime.

Emilie Gallant

In "The Missing Peace," she is a young American woman looking for her mother's remains in Haiti.

Isabelle Grant

In "The Missing Peace," she was a journalist and the mother of Emilie. Emilie believes she was killed during the night of the coup because she believed in the old regime.

Princesse

The protagonist of "Seeing Things Simply," she models for Catherine's nude portraits.

The old man

In "Seeing Things Simply," he is an old man who habitually gets drunk and talks to Princesse on her way to and from Catherine's house.

Catherine

In "Seeing Things Simply," she is a painter from Guadeloupe who makes nude portraits and sells them in Europe.

Suzette

The protagonist in "New York Day Women," she sees her mother walking through an unfamiliar part of New York City and decides to follow her.

Suzette's mother

In "New York Day Women," she is Suzette's mother. Though she longs for Haiti, she has yet to return because of the death and loss that await her there.

The child

In "New York Day Women," he is a young boy whom Suzette's mother babysits in park while his mother goes for a jog.

Grace/Gracina

The protagonist in "Caroline's Wedding," she is the older sister of Caroline and was born in Haiti. At the beginning of the short story, she has successfully acquired her U.S. citizenship.

Caroline

The sister of Grace in "Caroline's Wedding," she is the titular character. She was born in the United States and has only one arm.

Hermine

In "Caroline's Wedding," she is the mother of Grace and Caroline and believes that Caroline is "settling" or "selling herself short" by marrying Eric.

Grace's Father

In "Caroline's Wedding," he is the dead father of Grace and Caroline, and Hermine's dead husband. He died of prostrate cancer ten years before the time of the short story.

Eric

In "Caroline's Wedding," he is Caroline's Bahamian boyfriend. Hermine doesn't approve of him because he is not Haitian and has a speech impediment.

Mrs. Ruiz

In "Caroline's Wedding," she is the Cuban neighbor of Grace and her family. She frequently holds large and loud family parties at her house.

Judge Perez

In "Caroline's Wedding," he is a judge friend of Eric's who officiates the wedding ceremony for Eric and Caroline.

Krik? Krak! Glossary

Manman

The Haitian Creole word for 'mother'

wanga

A charm or spell

Fort Dimanche Prison

A former prison that was located in Port-au-Prince, infamous for its torture and murder of inmates during the regime of François Duvalier

indigent

A needy person

macoutes

A special operations unit within the Haitian military that François Duvalier created to increase his own power

genteel

To be polite or refined in an ostentatious way

gourdes

The current currency of Haiti

Ginen

In the Vodou religion, it is a forested island at the bottom of cosmic waters where the Iwa, the holy spirits of Vodou, reside

transistor

A type of radio

vagabonds

A wanderer, a person without a real home or connections

poupou

Feces or waste

kriz

A seizure

banyan

A type of fig that grows into a tree by growing on other plants

Lougarou

A mythical creature that flies at night by either turning into a bird or by taking off its skin and turning into a ball of fire

herring

A type of fish commonly eaten around the world

gendarme

A member of a military force that has assumed the policing duties of a civilian population

lago

A Haitian slang word for 'hide-and-seek'

jalousies

Window blinds or shutters that are made from rows of angled slats

madrigals

A song type dating back to the Renaissance and Early Baroque periods

bougainvillea

A genus of vines, bushes, and trees that have leaves near their flowers

manbos

The highest level of female clergy in the Vodou religion, tasked with maintaining the relationship between the spirits and the community

rara

A type of festival music that originated in Haiti and is typically used in street parades

merengue

A type of Carribbean dance normally associated with Haiti or the Dominican Republic.

posterity

A noun that refers to all future generations of people

dissonant

Clashing or lacking in harmony

frankfurter

A seasoned beef or pork sausage that has origins in Germany

bolero

A type of Spanish song or dance

calabash

A type of squash that can be harvested while still young and made into a bottle, utensil, pipe, etc.

Krik? Krak! Themes

Brutality

The brutal treatment the Haitian military metes out to the Haitian people is one of the driving forces of *Krik? Krak!* It breaks apart families, tears lovers asunder, forces characters to make difficult decisions, and causes them to question their allegiance to their mother country. The male letter writer in "Children of the Sea" is forced to abandon his love and flee to the United States because he fears the macoutes will torture and kill him. Those same macoutes brutally beat Madan Roger with the butts of their guns because of her son's connection to an anti-Duvalier radio show. Madan Roger's neighbors keep silent while she is beaten, even though it "sounds like [the soldiers] are cracking all the bones in her body," because they fear becoming the target of such violence themselves (Danticat 14). These are two clear examples of how brutal acts are used to keep the Haitian people within the government's control.

The brutality of the government and military is not only physical. It also has elements of psychological warfare. For example, Guy, from "A Wall of Fire Rising," commits suicide and abandons his wife and young son because he can no longer handle living in a corrupt military state devoid of freedom and opportunities. Another harrowing example of the mental and emotional manipulation of the Duvalier regime is the forced copulation of immediate family members. In "Children of the Sea" Célianne is forced to watch as the macoutes make her brother have sex with their mother. This type of senseless brutality is what causes Haitians like the Aziles from "Caroline's Wedding" to flee Haiti and question whether or not they should even go back to visit.

Hope

Because of the major and minor horrors and obstacles of daily life under the Duvalier regimes, the characters of *Krik? Krak!* continually oscillate between hope and hopelessness. Some, like Guy in "A Wall of Fire Rising" or Célianne in "Children of the Sea," succumb to the hopelessness of their situations and seek out freedom in the form of death. Others, like Lamort from "The Missing Peace," rally in the face of violence and maintain their hope. The source of this hope comes in different forms. For Lamort, her hope stems from her ability to finally claim her mother's name as her own. For Suzette in "New York Day Women," hope comes in the form of her stoutly Haitian mother learning how to navigate and survive in New York City.

Hope is also a weapon the Duvalier regime uses against the Haitian people. In "Children of the Sea" a rumor is circulated that the old president is returning. Thousands of Haitians flock to the airport to greet him, only to be gunned down and arrested by the macoutes. In a world where violence happens as quickly as taking a breath, hope can be a dangerous emotion to have.

National Identity

Questions and conflicts about national identity permeate all of the stories in *Krik? Krak!* Because of the injustice and terror the Duvaliers mete out to the Haitian people, some Haitians flee to the United States in search of safety, freedom, and opportunities. Once there, they grapple with the cultural differences between Haiti and the United States, and cling to some facets of their old lives despite their new surroundings. For example, Suzette's mother in "New York Day Women" refuses to go out to dinner, and prefers to cook meals at home. In "Caroline's Wedding," Hermine bemoans the fact that her daughters think and act "so American" and have "no taste buds" by her Haitian standards (Danticat 140). However, when Grace successfully becomes a naturalized citizen, Hermine is overjoyed, because it feels like the hopes and dreams she and her husband had of a better life in the United States have finally come to fruition. The desire to assimilate to American society while also maintaining their Haitian roots is one of the major conflicts facing the characters of *Krik? Krak!*

Furthermore, conflicts over national identity are not limited to exchanges between Haitians and Americans in *Krik? Krak!* Haiti has a tumultuous history with the Dominican Republic–a history that is heavily alluded to in "Nineteen Thirty-Seven." The murder and forced removal of Haitians from Dominica made many people question where their true home was, and what their real nationality was. Another example of this facet of struggles with national identity is found in "Caroline's Wedding." Hermine is deeply troubled that Caroline will marry Eric, a Bahamian, instead of a Haitian man. Although Eric is also from the Caribbean and an immigrant, the cultural differences his national identity represents are problematic to Hermine.

Love

The enduring power of love appears in many forms and from a plethora of sources in *Krik? Krak!* The love between lovers, of a father for his daughter, a mother for her son, strangers for strangers, etc. add an element of hope in the face of the trials and tribulations the characters must endure. In "Children of the Sea," the love of the two letter writers is shown in their commitment to write letters to each other, although they know those letters will never be sent or received. Also in "Children of the Sea," the father of the female letter writer forfeits all of his assets, his entire inheritance from his ancestors, in order to save his daughter from the macoutes. This type of sacrifice is also a form of love. The night woman in "Night Women" fights to shield her son from the truth about her status as a sex worker, because she wishes to preserve his innocence. This is also an act of love. Finally, the love strangers can have for strangers is apparent in "Between the Pool and the Gardenias," when Marie "adopts" Rose after finding the little baby girl abandoned near a sewer. Although Marie is in part motivated by her inability to have her own child, she still shows a willingness to nurture a baby who was cast out by its true parents. The love Marie harbors for Rose hints at the idea of a universal love Haitians have for one another.

Mother-Daughter Relationships

The relationships between mothers and daughters are at the crux of most of the tales in *Krik? Krak!* Mothers sacrifice themselves for their daughters, sometimes giving their lives for their daughters, and other times making difficult decisions so their daughters can have better futures. In "Nineteen Thirty-Seven," Défilé's mother is a prime example of a mother that sacrificed herself for her child. During the mass execution the Dominican Republic carried out against Haitians at the Massacre River Défilé's mother stayed behind so Défilé and her unborn child, Josephine, could escape. Défilé was forced to watch from the other side of the river as El Generalissimo's soldiers cut up her mother's body and threw it in the river. Later that same night, Défilé gave birth to Josephine. Rather than be traumatized that her mother's death is so clearly linked to her daughter's birth, Défilé tells Josphine, "at least you came out at the right moment to take my mother's place" (Danticat 36). It is evident from this quote that Défilé sees her mother and her daughter as two entities cut from the same biological and emotional cloth. Though she has lost her mother, she now has her daughter to fill the void in her life that her mother left.

The act of fleeing Haiti for a better life is also an example of a mother's sacrifice for her children. In "New York Day Women" and "Caroline's Wedding," we are presented with two older Haitian women who have varying degrees of difficulty adapting and assimilating to their new American surroundings. While these women undoubtedly fled Haiti in fear of the oppressive Duvalier regimes, they also left because they wanted to provide lives of opportunity for their daughters. This is felt most strongly in "Caroline's Wedding," when Grace finally earns her American citizenship and her mother rejoices at the "boundless possibilities" her daughter now has (Danticat 139).

Of course, the mother-daughter relationship is a two-way street. Daughters sacrifice for and nurture their mothers, while also challenging the long-held beliefs of the earlier generation. In "Nineteen Thirty-Seven," Josephine frequently visits her mother in jail despite the emotional pain it gives her and the danger of also being accused of witchcraft. In "The Missing Peace," Lamort fills the void her dead mother left in her grandmother's life. This is a clear parallel to Défilé and Josephine's situation in "Nineteen Thirty-Seven." In "Caroline's Wedding," Grace and Caroline provide for their mother's livelihood, while also challenging her traditional Haitian beliefs by questioning the restorative powers of strong bone soup and marrying a non-Haitian man. Throughout *Krik? Krak!* mothers and daughters (and grandmothers) perform roles in each other's lives that no one else could satisfy. The matrilineal lines and connections in *Krik? Krak!* run deep and strong.

Freedom

Freedom is an elusive idea and state of being in *Krik? Krak!* For some characters, like the male letter writer in "Children of the Sea," freedom means safety from political prosecution and the right to intellectual freedom. For the female inmates in "Nineteen Thirty-Seven," freedom means the end of their incarceration and the physical release of their bodies back into society. For Guy in "A Wall of Fire Rising," freedom means living life on his own terms and leaving behind a memory of himself he can be proud of. In all of these examples, the characters at first try to seek out freedom in the land of the living: the letter writer embarks on a dangerous exodus via boat in search of political asylum in the United States; the female inmates try to survive and scrape out existences for themselves while behind bars; and Guy tries to make the most of his life with his wife and son, often taking degrading jobs in order to support them. But despite their efforts, for all of these characters the type of freedom they seek is impossible to achieve. A sinking ship, disease, starvation, personal demons, etc. all bar their paths to freedom. So, in various ways, all of them succumb to death and find a different sort of freedom.

Mysticism

Elements of mysticism and the supernatural pervade almost every story in *Krik? Krak!* Sometimes there are direct references to magic, such as the female letter writer in "Children of the Sea" wishing she had wanga magic to use against the macoutes. Other times, the mysticism is present in the overall atmosphere, mood, and tone of the story. This is true in "Between the Pool and the Gardenias," when Marie is so transfixed at the thought of having her own baby that she ignores Rose's lack of life. As readers, we are left to wonder for most of "Between the Pool and the Gardenias" if Rose is actually still alive, or if Marie is hallucinating or performing magic that animates Rose. It is not until Marie remarks on Rose's increasing smell that we realize the baby is indeed dead. This inability to discern between life and death adds to the mystical, supernatural vibe of *Krik? Krak!*

At times the mysticism of *Krik? Krak!* is matter-of-fact and treated as mundane, while at other times it is a source of fear and persecution. For example, in "Seeing Things Simply," when a man buries his dead rooster as a sacrifice to his father, no one is alarmed, aside from remarking that he just wasted good meat. This wildly contrasts with what happens to Josephine's mother in "Nineteen Thirty-Seven," after she is accused of being a Lougarou. The difference in treatment of men who actually practice Voudou and women who are only *suspected* of practicing it reveal a gender bias and inequality *vis-à-vis* magic and mysticism in Haiti.

Krik? Krak! Quotes and Analysis

They treat Haitians like dogs in the Bahamas, a woman says. To them, we are not human. Even though their music sounds like ours. Their people look like ours. Even though we had the same African fathers who probably crossed these same seas together.

Unknown, "Children of the Sea," p.15

National identity and the divisions it can create between people is a key theme of *Krik? Krak!,* as proven by this quote. The speaker is lamenting the fact that, despite their cultural and physical similarities, Bahamians are antagonistic towards Haitians because of their different nationalities. As the speaker notes, because of the origins and history Haitians and Bahamians share, it is in part a twist of fate that some of their ancestors ended up in Haiti and others in the Bahamas. For such a random occurrence to have such significance is ironic. It is also indicative about the importance of national identity and national borders in our world.

Beloved Haiti, there is no place like you. I had to leave you before I could understand you.

Passengers on the boat, "Children of the Sea," p.10

An excerpt from a song about Haiti, this quote illustrates the complicated relationship the characters of *Krik? Krak!* have with their mother country. Haiti is their home, a place they love and cherish. The fraught political situation, however, makes it difficult and/or impossible for them to stay there. So they must leave their beloved country without fully understanding why she (i.e. Haiti) is simultaneously beautiful and dangerous, loving and hateful.

Someone says, Krik? You answer, Krak! And they say, I have many stories I could tell you, and then they go on and tell these stories to you, but mostly to themselves.

Male letter writer, "Children of the Sea," p.15

The title of *Krik? Krak!* is explained in this quote. The reader learns that “Krik?” and “Krak!” is an exchange between a would-be storyteller and their audience. It is interesting to note that the storyteller is reciting the tale for herself as well as for the listeners. This suggests that the act of telling a story is therapeutic and beneficial for both the teller and the listener.

At least I gave birth to my daughter on the night that my mother was taken from me...At least you came out at the right moment to take my mother's place.

Défilé, "Nineteen Thirty-Seven," p.34

The strong generational ties between mothers and daughters are on full display in this quote. When Défilé lost her mother at the Massacre River she lost one of her earthly tethers. She feels alone and abandoned, and thus when her daughter is born shortly after her mother's death, she no longer feels so lonely. The loss of her mother and the gain of her daughter occur so close in time that they feel linked. Her daughter replaces her mother and the cycle of close mother-daughter bonds continue.

Pretend that this is the time of miracles and we believed in them. I watched the owner for a long time, and I think I can fly that balloon. The first time I saw him do it, it looked like a miracle, but the more and more I saw it, the more ordinary it became.

Guy, "A Wall of Fire Rising," p.52

This excerpt demonstrates the importance of the hot air balloon to Guy, and it conveys the overall message of "A Wall of Fire Rising." The balloon symbolizes the audacity of hope in the face of impossible odds. Here is Guy, an impoverished man with no flight experience, thinking that flying the hot air balloon is something he can achieve. As he says, at first it seemed like an impossible task, but over time his confidence in his abilities grew. Guy's belief in his ability to fly the balloon despite his circumstances is a prime example of the hope prevalent throughout *Krik? Krak!*

You know that question I asked you before...how a man is remembered after he's gone? I know the answer now. I know because I remember my father, who was a very poor struggling man all his life. I remember him as a man that I would never want to be.

Guy, "A Wall of Fire Rising," p.54

The foreshadowing is strong in this excerpt from "A Wall of Fire Rising." These are the last words Guy says to Lili before he takes the Assads' hot air balloon and commits suicide. Guy reminisces about his father's life of drudgery and says he never wanted to be like his father. Unfortunately, the lack of opportunities in his community means that Guy struggles to make ends meet. Rather than live as his father did, he decides to end his life, an act foreshadowed in his last words to his wife.

One day you will stick your hand in a stew that will burn your fingers.

Lamort's grandmother, "The Missing Peace," p.95

This is a Haitian proverb that cautions against reckless behavior. Lamort's grandmother believes that Lamort takes too many risks and should be more cautious, especially with regards to her relationships with Toto and Raymond. When Lamort says she will help Emilie and answer all her questions, her grandmother uses this adage because she fears Lamort will get herself into trouble.

> *Why should we give to Goodwill when there are so many people back home who need clothes? We save our clothes for the relatives in Haiti.*
>
> *Suzette's mother, "New York Day Women," p.131*

This quote is significant because it illustrates the strong, enduring ties between Haiti and the country's emigrant people. Even though Suzette and her mother have not returned to Haiti since leaving it many years ago, Suzette's mother still has an emotional connection to and feels responsible for the loved ones still living in the Caribbean country.

> *In my family, we have always been very anxious about our papers.*
>
> *Grace, "Caroline's Wedding," p.139*

"Papers" is a colloquial term used for proof of citizenship documents, green cards, passports, visas, etc. For immigrants, "papers" are essential and can be the difference between a successful life in a new country or deportation. This is why Grace says that "papers" have always been a source of anxiety for her immigrant family.

> *I couldn't help but feel as though she was divorcing us, trading in her old allegiances for a new one.*
>
> *Grace, "Caroline's Wedding," p.139*

The bonds between mothers, daughters, grandmothers, and sisters are central to *Krik? Krak!* and are one of the major recurring themes of the collection. The mother-daughter bond is tested in "Caroline's Wedding" when Caroline goes against the wishes of her mother and marries Eric. In this quote, it seems that Caroline's wedding is also testing the relationship between her and her sister. Evidently, Grace feels as if Caroline is abandoning them by getting married. In her mind, Caroline cannot be allied to her mother and her sister while also being attached to her husband.

Krik? Krak! "Children of the Sea" Summary and Analysis

Summary

"Children of the Sea" opens with an undisclosed man writing a letter to his beloved. Currently at sea on a boat with 36 other people, he looks at the sky and relives memories from their childhood. Looking around the boat, he notes that its sails are white bed sheets spotted with blood. They remind him of loss of innocence and his lover's refusal to have sex with him. He tells her he was fine with her decision and that he just wanted to be close to her. The man ruefully remarks that his lover's father will probably marry her off, now that he (i.e. her lover) is gone. He begs her not to marry a soldier, because "they're almost not human" (Danticat 2).

Back in Haiti, the female letter writer despairs about her life. The sound of bullets floods the streets day and night. The schools have closed, the old president has fled, and the army has taken over. No one dares to leave their house. The girl's father orders her to destroy tapes from the male letter writer's controversial radio show, but she keeps a few. The other members of the male letter writer's youth federation group have disappeared, and are presumed to be either dead or in prison. It becomes clear that the male letter writer fled Haiti via boat in order to avoid the same fate. His lover shares that she no longer draws butterflies because black ones warn of death.

The man reveals that their boat is bound for America, specifically Miami. He wonders how much farther they have to go and prays that they don't hit a storm. He also writes about the other people onboard the boat. One of them is a pregnant girl with razor mark scars on her face. Seeing her makes the male letter writer happy that there aren't young children on the boat, because it would break his heart, "looking into their empty faces" and remembering "the hopelessness of the future" in Haiti (Danticat 3). Other characters aboard include some Protestants who see themselves as Job or the Children of Israel. They say, "the Lord gives and the Lord takes away," which causes the male letter writer to ask what more there is to take from him (Danticat 4).

Meanwhile in Haiti, the bodies of the male letter writer's fellow radio personnel have been released. Madan Roger, the neighbor of the female letter writer and her family, goes to collect her son's body. All that remains his head. To show what was done to her son, she carries the head all over Port-au-Prince. Once she arrives home, the macoutes stationed outside of her house taunt her and ask if the head is for her dinner. It takes a crowd of people to stop Madan Roger from attacking the militiamen. The female letter writer says events like this make her want to never leave the house again. She wishes there was a way she could know for certain if the male letter writer made it out of Haiti safely. She promises to continue writing the letters so that when they are reunited it will be as if they lost no time.

The first real day at sea sets in. Everyone onboard is sick, and their skin begins to burn from the sun. One man laments that soon they will be too dark to be mistaken for Cubans. The last time he tried to escape, he was on a boat with Cubans. Once they met with the US Coast Guard, the Cubans were taken to Miami while the Haitians were sent back to Haiti.

The pervasive smell of the sea is causing nausea. The male letter writer says it may be hard for his lover to understand, since she was raised in a "well-guarded house" with her genteel parents (Danticat 6). He's jealous of her upbringing, and thinks that perhaps if his upbringing were similar then he wouldn't have gotten caught up in Haiti's political troubles. The pregnant woman, whose name is Célianne, is ironically the only one unaffected by the sea smell. She eats nothing and just stares into space, rubbing her belly. One night she wakes up screaming because the boat is leaking under her sleeping spot. The captain of the vessel plugs up the boat with some tar and hopes that the Coast Guard finds them soon.

The father of the female letter writer discovers that she didn't destroy all of the radio tapes. He yells at his daughter, accusing her of being crazy and selfish. The female letter writer argues, and the situation escalates until the man begins to slap his daughter. Finally the girl's mother steps in and takes her husband away. The female letter writer wishes one of the macoutes' bullets would hit her.

The tar is holding up and there haven't been any new leaks in the boat in 2 days. The male letter writer's skin has turned very dark. He tries to buy a hat from one of the women on the boat with his remaining Haitian currency, but his money is worthless out in the middle of the ocean. The man realizes that he forgot where he was. He frequently dreams about a heaven that's at the bottom of the sea. In one of these dreams, his lover was there with his family. He tried to speak to her, but only bubbles came out of his mouth.

If he could talk to the female letter writer, he would hear of the new atrocities being committed in Haiti. The macoutes are forcing mothers and sons, fathers and daughters, to sleep with one another. There are already stories of young women carrying their father's children. The father of the female letter writer lives in fear of this happening to his family and plans for them to flee Port-au-Prince for Ville Rose.

The woman is still not speaking to her father because she thinks he's partly to blame for the forced exile of her lover. Her mother tries to intervene and explains that her father never approved of the male letter writer because the young man wasn't a social climber: he couldn't provide anything for the female letter writer that she didn't already have. The girl reasons that all she wants in a mate is love.

On the boat they are telling more stories and the male letter writer explains how the "Krik? Krak!" exchange works: someone proposes to tell a story by saying 'Krik?', and the audience accepts by answering 'Krak!'. They also listen to Bahamian radio stations using a transistor someone brought along. A woman says they treat Haitians like dogs in the Bahamas, even though they look the same and "had the same African fathers who probably crossed the seas together" (Danticat 8). The male lover wonders if the sea every ends, or if it's endless, like his love for his beloved.

One night the macoutes go to Madan Roger's house to interrogate her about her son's involvement with the youth federation. At first the woman refuses to tell them anything, instead insulting the men and their mothers. However, the macoutes are relentless with their questions, and eventually Madan Roger caves. The men begin to beat her brutally with their guns, cracking her bones. The mother of the female letter writer tells her husband that he should go help Madan Roger, but he refuses. He says that tomorrow they will leave Port-au-Prince, and they cannot jeopardize their own safety. He argues that what is happening now has happened before in Haiti, and it will happen again.

The next day, a rumor is circulated that the old president is coming back. People are rushing to the airport to meet him. The female letter writer's father says they will not stay behind in Port-au-Prince to see if this is true or not. Her mother says that the people going to the airport are "just too hopeful, and sometimes hope is the biggest weapon of all" (Danticat 10). Her father is determined to get his family to safety, and races out of the city.

Célianne has a beautiful baby girl, but the baby has yet to cry. The other passengers are calling the baby 'Swiss', because that was the word written on the knife they used to cut its umbilical cord. They also begin to speculate about how Célianne got pregnant in the first place. The boat has begun to crack heavily, and water is seeping in steadily. Nonessential belongings are thrown overboard to lighten the load. The captain whispers that something may have to be done with the people that never fully recovered from their seasickness.

The mother of the female letter writer turns out to be right: the old president didn't return, and the people who went to greet him at the airport were arrested and shot at by the military. During dinner one night, the female letter writer tells her father that she loves the male letter writer. He says nothing in response and finishes his meal. Later on, the female letter writer and her mother talk about love, family, and relationships. The mother tells her daughter that sometimes you must choose between your father and the man you love. The woman learns that her own father was a simple gardener from Ville Rose and did not have the approval of his wife's family when he married her.

Back on the boat, Célianne refuses to toss the body of her stillborn baby overboard. The male letter writer finally asks Célianne about the baby's father, and she shares the horrific story. One night a group of macoutes came to her home where she lived with her mother and brother. They forced her brother to have sex with their mother at gunpoint, then tied Célianne up and took turns raping her. When they were done, they arrested her brother for committing moral crimes and took him away. He was never heard from again. That same night Célianne cut up her face to hide her identity. She didn't know she was pregnant until her belly began to grow. She heard about the vessel leaving for the United States and decided to join it.

In Ville Rose, the female letter writer is finally settling in. There are many butterflies in the area, but none of them has landed on her hand; she hope this is a sign that her lover is safe. Her mother shares with her why her father has been so surly lately. The macoutes were going to come for the female letter writer and accuse her of being a member of the youth federation. In order to save her life, her father sold all of his land and property, including his inheritance from his own father, and gave the money to the macoutes. The female letter writer has no words, and doesn't know how she can thank her father for his sacrifice.

On the boat, Célianne finally throws her baby's corpse overboard. Shortly after it sinks below the waves, she jumps in after it, committing suicide. Everyone is in shock, but fear of the sharks in the area prevents a rescue mission. Besides, the boat is flooding in earnest now, the tar no longer holding up. Everything must go, including the notebook the male letter writer has been using for his letters. Though the other passengers remain hopeful that the Coast Guard will find them before the boat sinks, the male letter writer isn't as optimistic. He imagines himself living as a child of the sea among others "who have escaped the chains of slavery to form a world beneath the heavens and the blood-drenched earth" (Danticat 29).

The female letter writer finally finds the words to thank her father for saving her life. As he waves away her gratitude, his hand moves quickly in the air, resembling a black butterfly. The woman tries to run away from the sight, but it is too late. The news comes via radio that another boat has sunk off the coast of the Bahamas.

Analysis

The first story in *Krik? Krak!*, "Children of the Sea" is a tale of loss and the everlasting power of love. It establishes the historical and political landscape in which most of the book's stories are set. Though no date is explicitly given, a plethora of little details sprinkled throughout the story, when considered within the context of Haitian history, suggest that the story takes place in 1957. The most important detail is the presence of the tonton macoutes. The militia of Haitian dictator François Duvalier, the macoutes helped Duvalier gain and hold onto power during the corrupt 1957 Haitian elections. Once Duvalier was elected to the presidency, the old president was ousted and fled Haiti. Anyone found to have materials supporting the old regime could be arrested and persecuted. That is why at the beginning of the story, the female letter writer and her parents destroy and/or hide their buttons and posters supporting the old president.

Life in Haiti under the Duvalier regime was violent and dehumanizing, a fact that is at the center of "Children of the Sea." Through the alternating perspectives of the narrators we hear stories of senseless violence and horror. Parents were forced to copulate with their children, mothers walked the streets with the dismembered heads of their children, people were bludgeoned to death with guns, etc. Above all, political and intellectual freedom were nonexistent, causing many Haitians to flee their homeland. As we see in the main storyline of "Children of the Sea," these dire circumstances heavily influenced the lives and decisions of Haitian people. Perhaps this will be a trend in all of the *Krik? Krak!* stories.

In addition to setting the scene, "Children of the Sea" also introduces many of themes that are present throughout *Krik? Krak!* The theme of brutality is central. The macoutes perform unconscionable and senseless acts of violence and terror on pedestrian Haitian people, purportedly for the sake of preserving power and order. While some Haitians, like the male letter writer, have the means to attempt fleeing the country, most must stay behind and withstand the atrocity. Some of them hope that things will improve, that the old president will return and end the violence. Unfortunately, events keep happening that suggest this hope is ill founded. For example, the male letter writer manages to board a boat to safety, but it begins to sink soon after departing. And yet, the other passengers remain hopeful that the Coast Guard will find them before they drown. This ability of characters to continue to hope in the face of adversity is another recurring theme of *Krik? Krak!*

The theme of love is exhibited in the refreshing structure of "Children of the Sea." The story is told in the alternating perspectives of two lovers. Driven apart by the man's anti-Duvalier radio show and the woman's disapproving father, they promise to write letters to each other. That way if they are reunited, it will be as if they were never apart. The writers have no way of knowing if they will ever be able to exchange letters. Despite the possible futility of the exercise, they continue to write, driven by their love for one another. This is just one example of love's many forms in *Krik? Krak!* Another is the love parents have for their children, such as Célianne's for her unborn baby and the love between the female letter writer and her father.

On the boat, the theme of national identity is also alluded to during conversations about the Bahamas and Cuba. Despite Haiti's geographical and cultural nearness to both of these countries, Bahamians, Cubans, and Haitians all see themselves as drastically different from each other. By highlighting these beliefs in her work, Danticat questions the importance we place on national identity and borders.

Aside from a multitude of themes, other literary elements used effectively in "Children of the Sea" include similes and exposition. Two particularly striking similes involve the macoutes and the male letter writer's love for his beloved. The macoutes are compared to vicious vultures that swarm around the Haitian people as if they are rotting carcasses ripe for devouring. And the male letter writer describes his love for the woman as being as endless as the sea. This is particularly poignant, considering it is the sea that keeps the star-crossed lovers apart. The exposition occurs when the male letter writer explains what "Krik?" and "Krak!" mean, and how they are used in the storytelling process. This is a key explanation, since the title of the work is *Krik? Krak!*

Krik? Krak! "Nineteen Thirty-Seven" Summary and Analysis

Summary

The narrator, a young woman named Josephine, sits in a rocking chair with a Madonna doll she inherited from her mother. The Madonna emits a perfect tear from its porcelain face, and Josephine wonders if that means her mother has died. Although her bones ache at the thought of going into Port-au-Prince, Josephine prepares to go visit her mother at the prison in the city. During her walk to the prison, an old woman selling leeches stops Josephine and asks to see the doll. She also asks the young woman where she's from, and Josephine tells her she is from Ville Rose, the city of painters, poets, and coffee. The old woman guesses that Josephine is heading to the prison to see an inmate, and offers to show her a place where she can buy food for inmates.

Josephine buys food for her mother and enters the prison. Built by American Marines during the 19-year occupation of Haiti by the United States, from the outside it is a solid and durable fort-like structure. Inside, the smell of the food Josephine bought mixes with the odor of urine and excrement. A few minutes after Josephine enters, her mother emerges from the depths like a ghost. She is skinnier than the last time her daughter visited her. Her skin hangs from her bones, "falling in layers, flaps, on her face and neck" (Danticat 34). These wrinkles are a source of suspicion for the prison guards, who believe they are the result of witchcraft. Josephine's mother was originally arrested on charges of dabbling in the occult, and has been sentenced to life in prison. When she dies, her remains are to be burned in the prison yard, to prevent her soul from entering a new body.

During her visit with her mother, Josephine doesn't speak. She simply gives her mother the Madonna doll and the food she brought. Her mother is thrilled to the see the doll and handles it very carefully. She asks if the doll has cried yet before breaking into sobs herself. A guard comes with a rifle and taps Josephine's mother in the torso so she'll stop crying. She complies, and puts on a brave smile. She tells Josephine that the guards haven't treated her horribly. They do shave her head every week, and force the other women prisoners to pour ice water on each other at night. This is to prevent the women from growing their wings of flames and escaping.

As Josephine and her mother sit quietly, the other female inmates begin to walk into the prison yard. They are all in various states of poor health and decay. Some have weeping scabs and bruises. They have all been accused of being witches, of "rising from the ground like birds on fire" (Danticat 36).

Thinking about these women reminds Josephine of the day her mother was arrested. They had just moved to Port-au-Prince and were staying at a friend's house. The friend's baby was sick from colic, and Josephine's mother helped look after it. One day, Josephine woke up to the sounds of a mob outside the house. Rushing out of the house, Josephine saw the mob hitting her mother with rocks and punches, and two policemen dragging her away. Amongst the mob was the friend with whom Josephine and her mother were staying. The woman had accused Josephine's mother of killing her baby and so the crowd had gathered together, calling Josephine's mother a lougarou, a witch, and a criminal. Josephine tried to break through the crowd, but it was too thick. All she could do was watch helplessly as her mother was dragged away.

The memory of her mother's arrest sparks another memory. This time, Josephine and her mother are at the Massacre River, where the soldiers of the Dominican Republic murdered thousands of Haitians, including Josephine's grandmother. In this memory Josephine's mother speaks to the river, thanking it for saving her from its womb, while Josephine was still in *her* womb. Josephine remembers visiting the river many times, occasionally with other women who had also lost their mothers there. For Josephine's mother, the river was where it all began. She says to Josephine, "at least I gave birth to my daughter on the night that my mother was taken from me" (Danticat 40).

Back in the present day, Josephine gets ready to leave the prison. Her mother promises to tell her the secret of how the Madonna cries, but Josephine already knows. Still, she humors her mother. When she tries to hug her mother goodbye, her mother pushes her away and tells her to visit again soon.

The next two visits are brief and troubling. Josephine's mother has developed a cough that she can't get rid of. Josephine wants to embrace her mother, but knows her mother will refuse because she fears giving her daughter one of the prison sicknesses. During the second visit, Josephine wants to break her silence with her mother, but cannot find the words. All her mother does is cry and act deliriously. She even refuses to hold the Madonna doll. When Josephine finally does speak to her mother, she asks, "Manman, did you fly?" (Danticat 42.)

A week later, a woman named Jacqueline comes to Josephine's house in Ville Rose in the middle of the night. She is dressed in all white and claims to have gone to the river with Josephine and her mother in the past. As a test, Josephine leads Jacqueline through a question-and-answer sequence that all daughters of the river know. Jacqueline passes, and tells Josephine that her mother is dying, if not already dead. The pair rushes to the prison in Port-au-Prince.

At the prison gate, the guard tells the women that the body of Josephine's mother is being prepared for the afternoon pyre. Josephine is frozen in shock and Jacqueline asks to be taken to the cell Josephine's mother lived in. In the cell are six other women, each wearing or holding something that belonged to Josephine's mother. The inmates tell Josephine that her mother was beaten to death in the prison yard because the guards did not know how to cure her sickness. They give Josephine a pillow filled with her mother's shorn off hair.

Josephine wants to leave, but Jacqueline says they should stay and watch her mother's body burned. Josephine says she would stay if she knew the truth about her mother's supposed ability to fly. Jacqueline asks if she never asked her mother about flying. This triggers a memory in Josephine. She remembers a story her mother told her about that day in 1937, the day of the massacre. Weighed down by Josephine's unborn body, her mother leapt from the Dominican side of the Massacre River to the Haitian side. The red water of the river, red from the blood of slain Haitians, clung to her body and looked like flames.

Back in the prison yard, Josephine holds the Madonna doll, looks toward the sun, and thinks that maybe one day she might see her mother there.

Analysis

A tale overflowing with mysticism and history, "Nineteen Thirty-Seven" illustrates the incarceration side of life in Haiti. Through the story of Josephine and her mother, Danticat shows what used to happen to powerful, strange, and unpopular women in Haiti. Wrongfully accused of killing her friend's baby, Josephine's mother is condemned as a witch, beaten in the streets, and sentenced to life in prison. Her *possible* connection to magic and the occult makes her a threat in the eyes of society. Judging from the intense feelings of the mob that beats Josephine's mother, magic and the supernatural are not topics to be tossed around and trifled with in Josephine's time. And yet, in "Children of the Sea," characters are almost flippant in their references to *wanga* magic and the like. This suggests that only certain types of people are automatically condemned when they are accused of using magic. Fatherless and husbandless, with presumably a dearth of money, Josephine and her mother are amongst society's vulnerable and thus cannot successfully challenge those who imprison Josephine's mother. While in other stories mysticism plays a more benign role, in "Nineteen Thirty-Seven" it is a knife that slices off the characters' wings.

The topic of wings and flight is pivotal to "Nineteen Thirty-Seven." In prison, Josephine's mother and the other inmates are doused nightly with cold water in order to prevent them from sprouting wings of fire and escaping. This myth that the female prisoners can fly is so pervasive that Josephine's own daughter asks her mother did she fly. Rather than say 'yes' or 'no', Josephine's mother gives a cryptic answer. It is only after her mother dies that Josephine recalls her mother did "fly" once. She "flew" across the Massacre River to escape the Dominican soldiers and emerged from the river with her blood-red wings. Of course, Josephine's mother did not actually flap wings like a bird does. However, to save herself and her unborn baby, she did have to soar through the air like a bird when she jumped from the Dominican side of the river to the Haitian side. It may not have been a literal flight, but it was a flight to freedom nonetheless.

In addition to the themes of mysticism and freedom, the theme of mother-daughter relationships is important in "Nineteen Thirty-Seven." Although they don't speak much during the final days of Josephine's mother's life, Josephine and her mother have an ironclad, undeniable bond. This bond began as the typical bond between a mother and her child, and was solidified by the blood of Josephine's grandmother during the events at Massacre River. Josephine's grandmother sacrificed herself so her daughter and unborn granddaughter could make it out of the Dominican Republic alive. Later that same day, shortly after her grandmother sacrificed herself, Josephine was born. In the words of Josephine's mother, Josephine "came out at the right moment to take [her] mother's place." (Danticat 40) From this quote it is clear that for Josephine's mother, Josephine fills the void her mother's death left. The Madonna, passed down from mother to daughter since the days of Josephine's great-great-great-grandmother, is a symbol of these strong generational mother-daughter relationships.

The plot of "Nineteen Thirty-Seven" also features an important and infamous episode from Haitian and Dominican history. This is the 1937 massacre of Haitians living in the Dominican Republic. The 5 days of killings were purportedly an attempt to root out migrant Haitian workers who worked in the sugar plantations along the Haitian-Dominican border. Once dead, the bodies of the murdered Haitians were dumped en masse into the Massacre River, a body of water separating the two countries. This is where the story of Josephine and her mother intersects with actual Haitian history.

The horrors and brutality of the 1937 massacre place "Nineteen Thirty-Seven" in a unique historical and political context. While the focus of "Children of the Sea" is primarily Haiti's internal strife, "Nineteen Thirty-Seven" shifts the gaze to Haiti's relationship with its neighbors.

Krik? Krak! "A Wall of Fire Rising" Summary and Analysis

Summary

Guy, Lili, and Little Guy live in a one-room shack in a shantytown in Haiti's countryside. Lili is a stay-at-home mother, Little Guy goes to school, and Guy works odd jobs. One day Guy comes home with news to tell. Before he can share his news, Little Guy says proudly that he was assigned the lead role in his school play. Lili encourages Little Guy to recite one of his monologues for his father. The play is about the Haitian revolutionary Dutty Boukman, and is full of passionate, fiery language. Little Guy gives a spirited performance for his parents, and their applause thunders in their little house.

The family eats their meager dinner of cornmeal mush and decides to go to the local sugar mill for entertainment. The government had installed a large television near the mill so that Haitians living in the shantytown could watch the state-sponsored news. Once the news finishes, people stay around to make bonfires and complain about the government. Over the past year, however, Guy and his family have found their own amusement. The Assads, the wealthy Haitian-Lebanese family that runs the sugar mill, have a hot air balloon from America that they fly in the skies above the shantytown. When not in use, the hot air balloon is locked away in a field surrounded by a chain link fence. While Lili and Little Guy enjoy looking at the balloon, Guy is completely obsessed with it. Lili is concerned about her husband's fascination with the balloon, but tries not to show it.

After stretching his hands through holes in the fence as if to touch the balloon, Guy stops and sits with his wife on the grass. He tells Lili that he knows he can make the balloon fly. Before Lili can question him further, Little Guy asks his father to play hide-and-seek with him. The father and son play until Guy becomes breathless. He sits down again next to Lili while Little Guy runs off. Guy begins to tell Lili about his news from earlier, but Little Guy runs up behind them and interrupts. When Lili announces that it is time to go home, Little Guy protests under his breath. His father squeezes his ear in punishment. Lili steps in, and Guy grows angry because he thinks she is undermining him. He storms off towards their house, and his family follows behind him.

At home, Lili puts Little Guy to bed and performs her nightly ablutions. Guy walks in and notes time's effects on his wife's body. The couple lies down on their sleeping mat and Guy is finally able to tell Lili his news. He was able to secure a few hours of work at the sugar mill. This is good news, because jobs at the mill are hard to come by. Lili wonders why Guy isn't more excited about the work, and he tells her it's because he will be scrubbing the latrines of the mill. Lili tries to console him, but Guy remains bitter. He is number 78 on the sugar mill's permanent job waiting list.

He muses aloud about whether he should put Little Guy's name on the list now, so that he will have a job once he's an adult. Lili protests, saying that she doesn't want to limit her son's future. Guy agrees to not put their son's name on the list.

Guy and Lili's conversation drifts back to the hot air balloon. Guy imagines himself flying the balloon, high in the sky like a bird. Lili tells him that if God wanted humans to fly, he would have given them wings. Guy agrees, but then wonders why God made the air and birds, because they make humans want to fly. Before Lili can respond, Little Guy screams and disturbs the peace of the night. He dreamt that he could not remember his lines. His parents help him remember and they all go to sleep.

The next evening, Little Guy comes home with more lines for his play. Guy is exhausted from his day working at the mill, but sits and listens to his son's oration. The speech is about freedom and liberation, and brings tears to Guy's eyes. He hugs his son, congratulations him on his success, and leaves the house.

After dinner, Lili takes Little Guy to the field because she knows that's where they can find Guy. Sure enough, Guy is sitting next to the fence with the hot air balloon. When Lili joins him on the grass, Guy tells her not to ask him about his day. He tells her that she will raise their son to be a performer. He says he wishes he could fly the hot air balloon to a place where he can build his own house. Lili says she wants him to stay away from the balloon from now on. She knows that she and Little Guy aren't included in his fantasies about it, and this scares her. Guy doesn't respond and falls asleep on top of her. When he wakes up, he asks her how a man is judged once he's gone. Lili replies that a man is judged by his deeds, and adds that their son has never gone to bed hungry. Just then, Little Guy runs up to them, and the little family goes home.

This time, Guy helps Lili with her nightly ritual. As he helps his wife rub lemon over her skin, Guy returns to their earlier discussion. He says he knows the answer to his question of how a man is remembered. He remembers his father, who was a struggling poor man his entire life. Guy remembers him as a man he would never want to be.

The next morning, Guy and Little Guy leave for work and school. Lili goes to the public water fountain with a few other women. On her way back, she sees a terrified Little Guy waiting for her at their house. At first she thinks her son forgot his lines again, but then Little Guy tells her that Guy has taken the balloon. The boy points to the sky as Guy sails over their heads in the balloon.

Lili and Little Guy go to the field by the sugar mill. A crowd has gathered to watch Guy fly the balloon. Among them is a member of the Assad family, who wonders how Guy is managing to fly the balloon by himself. Suddenly, the crowd begins to scream because it looks like Guy is going to jump from the balloon. Lili hides Little Guy's face in her skirt as her husband hurtles through the air. Guy hits the ground not far from the gathered crowd and immediately begins to bleed out. Assad goes to check for a pulse, but Guy is already dead. The hot air balloon continues to float along and disappears into the distance.

Lili and Little Guy rush over to Guy's body. Workers from the sugar mill come with a cot and blanket for the body. As they drape the cloth over Guy's body, Little Guy begins to recite another line from his play. Lili asks to look at her husband's face for one last time. She traces her husband's features with her eyes, looking for something that could remind her of the man she had married. One of the workers asks if she wants to close Guy's eyes. Lili says no, because her husband liked to look at the sky.

Analysis

The title of "A Wall of Fire Rising" comes from a line in the play in which Little Guy is acting. The play is about Dutty Boukman, a Haitian revolutionary who helped Haiti gain its independence from France. Various monologues from the play are scattered throughout "A Wall of Fire Rising," imbuing the story's atmosphere with fire and passion. The inclusion of a figure like Boukman in a story that already resonates with feelings of freedom and hope helps to solidify these themes in the work.

All three of the main characters in "A Wall of Fire Rising" have freedom on their minds. For Little Guy, wide-eyed and innocent, freedom is a concept dicussed in his play. While it's fun to memorize lines about freedom and perform for his family, he doesn't have a clear idea about what freedom actually means. For Guy and Lili, however, freedom is a more complicated topic. Guy struggles daily to provide for his family. The lack of job opportunities in their town means that some nights the family survives on flavored water for sustenance. For him, freedom means being able to earn a livelihood for his family. He fears being like his own father, who was a struggling and poor man his entire life. As time goes on and Guy's job prospects don't improve, he begins to turn to the Assads' hot air balloon for solace. Lili recognizes that her husband is increasingly obsessed with the hot air balloon. She fears that in his search for freedom Guy will leave her and Little Guy behind. Her fears prove to be well founded when Guy commits suicide.

Besides being a major source of conflict in the story and the vehicle of Guy's suicide, the hot air balloon is also a symbol of freedom, hope, class, and economic prosperity. It is no coincidence that the Assads, the wealthy owners of the most profitable business in town, own the hot air balloon. As a quirky piece of technology from America, the balloon personifies decadence, excess wealth, and exclusivity. The inhabitants of the shantytown know that the hot air balloon is something they can never hope to own. Guy frequently fantasizes about using the hot air balloon to fly away from his responsibilities and the harsh realities of his life. For him, the hot air balloon represents his hopes for a better future. During one of his fantasies, the hot air balloon takes him to a place where he is free to build his own house–it literally acts as his vehicle to freedom. That is why at the end of the story he uses the balloon to commit suicide and escape from his earthly shackles. Perhaps in his mind committing suicide was his only means of achieving freedom.

Guy's plan with the hot air balloon is heavily foreshadowed. During his last evening with his family he repeatedly tells Lili that she will take good care of Little Guy, that she will make a performer out of him. His use of "you" and not "we" in his statements about their son's future is the first red flag. The second comes when he actually vocalizes to Lili his dreams of flying away in the balloon. Poor Lili doesn't know that she should take his fantasies seriously. The last major piece of foreshadowing is Guy's discussion of his father. He tells Lili that growing up, he never wanted to be like his father, who was "a very poor struggling man all his life" (Danticat 75). And yet, here he is, living in a one-room shanty house, struggling to put food in the mouths of his family. It is not Lili's fault that she didn't realize Guy's feelings about living in poverty would drive him to take his own life. Rather, these indicators leading up to Guy's suicide shows how resolute he was in his decision.

Unlike "Children of the Sea" and "Nineteen Thirty-Seven," "A Wall of Fire Rising" is less about Haiti's politics and more about quotidian Haitian life. Haiti's political, social, and economic struggles do play a part in the story's events, but they form the backdrop of the drama and do not take center stage. Rather, it is the little triumphs and tragedies of Guy, Lili, and Little Guy that are the focus of the story. This change in scope from the macro to the micro level is partly what makes *Krik? Krak!* a diverse collection of stories.

Krik? Krak! "Night Women" Summary and Analysis

Summary

A 25-year-old woman sits in the dark and watches her son prepare for bed. A curtain splits their one-room house into two separate spaces. The shadow of her son against the curtain reminds the woman of her son's father, an old lover who disappeared years ago. As the boy tucks himself into bed, he wraps his mother's red scarf around his neck. This is the scarf the woman uses to attract her nighttime patrons.

The woman is a prostitute, a woman stuck between the daytime and the nighttime. During the day she tempts men and at night they come to her house. In order to keep her activities a secret from her son, the woman put up the curtain to separate his bed from hers. Before she lets in her suitors, she blows on his eyelashes and touches his face to make sure he is truly sleeping.

Tonight, a doctor named Emmanuel is the visitor. He comes every Tuesday and Saturday and brings flowers. He has a wife, but claims that she isn't as beautiful as the night woman. On Mondays and Thursdays, Alexandre the accordion player is the visitor. He likes to make accordion sounds in the night woman's ear when they lie together. Now with the doctor, the night woman takes pains to make sure they don't wake up her son. If the boy does wake up and see them, she is prepared to tell him that the ghost of his father has returned from heaven.

She doesn't need this fabrication tonight, though. She and Emmanuel finish their business, and he leaves at dawn. Before he goes, he calls the night woman an avalanche and a waterfall.

After he leaves, the night woman sits outside and smokes a dry tobacco leaf. She watches a group of women walk towards the marketplace and thanks the stars that her days are her own. She goes back into the house and hears her son waking up. He asks her if he has missed the angels. She slips into his bed, tells him the angels have a lifetime to visit them, and then she rocks him back to sleep.

Analysis

A very short story, "Night Women" has a dreamlike feel to it. This is partly because most of the story's content consists of stream-of-consciousness-like observations and musings from the narrator. Her mind jumps from one subject to the next, and she sometimes spirals into tangents. This is similar to how the content, setting, and/or characters in a dream can quickly change. For example, one moment the night woman is thinking about a firefly that is buzzing around her house, and the next moment she is likening love to a childhood lesson about shoes.

The use of ephemeral imagery and figurative speech further develops the hazy, dreamlike atmosphere of the story. The woman describes how shadows "shrink" and "spread" over the curtain dividing her and her son (Danticat 81). For a brief moment, her son's shadow stretches into the silhouette of a grown man, before shrinking back to his own size. When describing herself, the woman says she is stuck in the brief time between day and night, in the fleeting moments of amber-colored twilight. Later on in the story, she compares her son to a fluttering butterfly that momentarily rests on a rock: at any moment, he could fly away from her.

The woman's love for her son fuels most of her actions. She has sex with strangers to provide for their living, at great risk to herself and her body. She tries her hardest to hide the truth of her nighttime activities from her son, in an attempt to preserve his innocence. All of these actions are acts of love. Although her vocation makes her stand out from other parents in the *Krik? Krak!* stories, the night woman's commitment to and love for her son remind us that she too is a mother trying to provide the best possible life for her child.

Krik? Krak! "Between the Pool and the Gardenias" Summary and Analysis

Summary

Marie is a young Haitian woman who works as a maid for a wealthy family in Pétion-Ville. While walking one day in Port-au-Prince, Marie stumbles upon a beautiful baby girl lying abandoned in the street. She is wearing a blue dress with the letters R-O-S-E embroidered on it, and so Marie decides to call her 'Rose'. Unlike other children, Rose doesn't stir or cry out. Her lips are wide and purple, and she smells like gardenias and fish. To Marie, who has suffered from multiple miscarriages, Rose is a gift from Heaven, much like Baby Jesus or Baby Moses. At first, she thinks the baby may be a trap from her "enemies," the women that sleep with her husband; however, she is so consumed with the idea of having her own child that she buries her suspicions and takes the baby home.

Marie frequently dreams about her dead mother and other dead women from her family. These women include Josephine's mother Défile from "Nineteen Thirty-Seven" and Lili from "A Wall of Fire Rising." Marie believes these women have "claimed her" because they want her to "do some good for somebody" (Danticat 92). Perhaps, she thinks, this "somebody" is baby Rose.

Back at home in Pétion-Ville, Marie hides Rose in the maid's room before rushing to prepare lunch for her employers. Called 'Monsieur' and 'Madame', they are bourgeois Haitians and call Marie a manbo, or Voudou priestess, behind her back. After she serves the meal, Marie lays Rose on the kitchen table and talks to the baby about her life. She explains why she left her home in Ville Rose and her husband after being married to him for ten years. Because she was unable to give her husband children, he cheated on her and had "ten different babies with ten different women" (Danticat 94).

Marie also tells the baby about her relationship with the Dominican man who cleans her employers' pool three times a week. She and the man slept together once, but haven't talked since then. Marie pretends that Rose is the baby of her and the Dominican, and that the three of them own her employer's house. Rose doesn't react to Marie's chattering, and Marie remarks that she is a perfect child. When Monsieur and Madame are finished eating, Marie takes Rose outside and sits with her in a rocking chair. She falls asleep in the chair with Rose in her arms.

The next day, Marie wakes up and Rose is still in her arms, as perfect as she was when Marie fell asleep. It is only three days later that Rose begins to smell. Marie compares the smell to rotting pig intestines and bathes the baby several times a day to keep the smell down. She even uses some of Madame's perfume, but it fails to keep the smell at bay. Marie wants to return Rose to where she found her, but feels responsible for the baby's soul. She begins to hide Rose in a shack behind the house, where the Dominican man keeps his tools. She visits her 3 times a day, and watches as Rose's body decomposes. When Rose begins to attract flies Marie realizes that it's time to let her go. She dresses the baby in a yellow dress she had sewn for her own miscarried babies, and goes to bury her.

Marie decides to bury Rose in the garden next to the pool. She puts her on the ground and digs a shallow grave next to the gardenias. As Marie is lowering Rose into the grave, she feels a grip on the shoulder. She turns around, expecting Madame, but it is the Dominican man. He asks her what she is doing as Rose slips out of her fingers and lands on the ground between them. Marie starts to explain, but the Dominican cuts her off. He says he knows Marie killed the baby and intends to use her for some evil purpose. He tells Marie that he has already notified the gendarmes. When Marie tries to reason with him, saying that he knows her, he retorts that he doesn't know her "from the fly on a pile of cow manure" and accuses her of eating little children (Danticat 97).

Marie knows resistance is futile. She looks down at Rose and sees in her mind all her miscarried babies. She waits for the gendarmes with Rose and the Dominican, between the pool and the gardenias.

Analysis

"Between the Pool and the Gardenias" is perhaps the most mysterious and mystical story in *Krik? Krak!* The source of much of the mystery and mysticism is Rose, the dead baby that Marie finds in the streets of Port-au-Prince. For most of the tale, it is not clear if Rose is dead or alive. Though Rose doesn't cry out or speak, Marie's treatment of her leads the reader to believe that perhaps she is still alive. After all, why would Marie take a dead baby home and care for it as if it were her own child? It is not until Marie mentions Rose's growing smell that the reader receives confirmation of Rose's mortality.

That confirmation introduces a whole slew of new questions and considerations. Are Marie's employers correct–is she actually a manbo? Does she intend to perform some sort of ritual to bring Rose back to life? Or is she a woman suffering from PTSD after her numerous miscarriages? Or perhaps she is so gripped by the desire to have a child that she hallucinates when she sees Rose's corpse. The story provides enough evidence to support any one of these theories. And yet, in the end, it doesn't really matter what Marie's intention or motivation was: if Défile's fate in "Nineteen Thirty-Seven" is any indication, the gendarmes will condemn Marie to a life behind bars no matter what she says. Unfortunately for Marie, the love she has and the care she gives to a complete stranger are her downfall.

Marie's dreams are the other source of mysticism in "Between the Pool and the Gardenias." In these dreams, Marie's mother, great grandmother, grandmother, and godmother visit her. These women are familiar to us, because they are characters from other *Krik? Krak!* stories. Marie's mother, grandmother, and great grandmother are Josephine, Défile, and Josephine's grandmother from "Nineteen-Thirty Seven," while Lili from "A Wall of Fire Rising" is Marie's godmother. All of these women are dead, but they reach through time and space to commune with Marie. How they are able to do this is not explained, which adds to the mystery and mysticism. Marie believes these women put Rose in her path so she could help the baby girl. She mentions them when she tries to justify her actions to the Dominican, which probably made her seem more culpable in his eyes.

The Dominican is an important piece of "Between the Pool and the Gardenias," and of the entire *Krik? Krak!* collection. Before his character appears, non-Haitians are only discussed in the abstract. In "Children of the Sea," Cubans are described as people who treat Haitians worse than dogs, while in "Nineteen Thirty-Seven" Dominicans are remembered as the perpetrators of a mass murder of Haitian people. "Between the Pool and the Gardenias" is the first time a person of a different nationality plays an influential role in the story's plot. The slightly antagonistic and complicated relationship between the Dominican and Marie suggests that not much has changed between Haiti and the Dominican Republic since 1937. Despite the fact that he and Marie were once intimate, the Dominican does not hesitate to report her to the authorities. He even claims that he doesn't know her anymore than he knows a fly on a dung heap. It is unclear if the difference in nationality contributed to the man's refusal to hear Marie's side of the story; however, it is important to highlight that the first non-Haitian character of the *Krik? Krak!* stories is in part responsible for the arrest of one of the main characters of the stories.

While mystery, mysticism, love, and national identity all play major roles in "Between the Pool and the Gardenias," imagery and parallelism are also important devices in the story. In the passages about Rose, Danticat uses rich sensory details to describe the baby's appearance, behavior, and smell. Descriptions of the last feature are particularly poignant; for instance Danticat compares Rose's decomposing body to the smell of rotting pig intestines (Danticat 98). Early on in the story, Baby Rose's situation is paralleled to that of Baby Moses or Baby Jesus. Like Moses, her birth parents abandoned her, and like Jesus, there was no one to kiss her in her final moments. The use of these literary elements adds texture to the story and helps to tell Marie's story more fully.

"Between the Pool and the Gardenias" is the first *Krik? Krak!* story to include people of different nationalities. It will be interesting to see if subsequent stories continue this trend.

Krik? Krak! "The Missing Peace" Summary and Analysis

Summary

The story opens with Raymond and Lamort playing in a field with leaves shaped like butterflies. Raymond is a young macoute and Lamort is a young woman living alone with her grandmother. Raymond is trying unsuccessfully to seduce Lamort, who distracts him by asking him to recount the story of how he got his limp. Raymond relishes the opportunity to show his bravery, and so tells Lamort the story again.

He was on guard the night of the regime change, but no one had told him about the coup in Port-au-Prince. Thus, Raymond was still wearing the old regime uniform when his friend Toto came up and saw how he was dressed. Toto didn't know if Raymond was part of the old or new regime, so he fired his gun at him. In the chaos of the moment Raymond forgot the password given to all soldiers. He finally remembered when one of Toto's bullets hit him in the leg. He yelled out the password and Toto stopped shooting.

Laughing, Lamort asks Raymond why he didn't just take off the uniform. He ignores the question, instead asking her if she remembers the password he told her. She whispers the password, 'peace', in his ear. Raymond tells her to never forget the password, because it may save her life one day. Just then, a round of gunshots resounds through the air, signaling the start of curfew. Lamort says goodbye to Raymond, who blows her a kiss and tells her to be careful.

On her way home, Lamort passes by the gutted, abandoned houses of old-regime followers. Many of them died the night of the coup, and those who survived fled to the hills or took boats to Miami. Seeing a bed of red hibiscus near the houses, Lamort stops and picks a few before continuing home.

Lamort's grandmother waits for her outside their house. She throws away Lamort's hibiscus, saying that they grow with blood on them. Lamort's grandmother has news to share. Someone has rented the yellow house they let, and she needs Lamort to bring their guest some needles and thread. Many of the visitors to Ville Rose choose to stay at their rental house, and it is always exciting. Lamort and her grandmother rush to make Lamort look presentable, scrubbing her skin with mint leaves and changing her clothes. Lamort's grandmother tells her that their guest is a foreign lady, Mademoiselle Grant, and that she shouldn't bother her unnecessarily. Lamort asks a plethora of questions about the guest, including if she is old regime or new regime. Her grandmother answers that the woman believes in God's regime, and that she is here to "write things down for posterity" (Danticat 104). Lamort tells her grandmother that if the woman asks her questions, she will answer them. Her grandmother warns her that she will get into trouble one day. Still, she sends her granddaughter off to their guest, after telling Lamort she looks as pretty as Lamort's mother used to.

Lamort arrives quickly at the yellow house and knocks on the door, calling out "Mademoiselle Grant" (Danticat 105). A young woman wearing jeans answers the door and asks Lamort how she knows her name. She lets Lamort into the house after Lamort says her grandmother sent her with the needles. The woman introduces herself as Emilie, and asks Lamort for her name. After Lamort introduces herself, Emilie asks how she came to be named 'death'. Lamort explains that her mother died while giving birth to her, and she was named for that.

Emilie gives Lamort lemonade and butter cookies, and lights a cigarette for herself. Lamort asks Emilie if she is a journalist, and Emilie says she isn't, she's just visiting people in the area. Lamort asks who these people are, but Emilie evades the question. Lamort continues to ask questions until Emilie says that Lamort is the true journalist. She asks if Lamort can read and write, to which Lamort replies that she can't read American. The words Emilie wanted Lamort to read were in French, which proves that Lamort is illiterate. Lamort is embarrassed, but Emilie tells her there is nothing to be ashamed of.

Evidently warming up to Lamort, Emilie reveals her true purpose for coming to Ville Rose. Her mother was old regime and a journalist working for newspaper called *Libéte* in Port-au-Prince. The last time Emilie's mother was heard from, she was reporting in this region of Haiti. Emilie suspects her mother may have been killed the night of the coup, and wants Lamort to take her to the mass burial site. She takes out several photos of her mother and asks if Lamort recognizes her. Lamort does not, but agrees to take Emilie to the gravesite.

Just then, Lamort's grandmother comes to the door. Lamort has to hide from her grandmother, or else she will not be able to take Emilie to the gravesite. She hides in Emilie's bedroom and sees a purple cloth spread over the bed with many patches of square cloth laid over it. Outside, Lamort's grandmother and Emilie make small talk before Lamort's grandmother asks about her granddaughter. Emilie lies and says Lamort already left. Lamort's grandmother doesn't believe her, but leaves anyways.

Emilie comes into the bedroom with a flashlight and an American passport. Lamort asks her what the cloth is for. Emilie tells her that it was her mother's dream to make a quilt using that purple cloth, and she wanted to fulfill that dream for her.

The pair prepares to leave for the churchyard. Lamort warns Emilie that the yard is guarded at night, and Emilie tells Lamort that the younger girl has a reputation: another journalist who stayed at the yellow house in the past told Emilie that Lamort would be willing to take her to the gravesite. Lamort takes the compliment in stride, and asks Emilie what she'll do if she finds her mother's remains. Emilie replies that she hadn't thought that far ahead yet, and remarks that Lamort was born a woman.

Lamort and Emilie walk silently through the night until they reach the gravesite. They have barely entered the yard when a voice calls out, "Who is there?" (Danticat

117.) Emilie announces herself as an American journalist to a solider holding blinding flashlight. The solider is Raymond's friend, Toto. In the night he doesn't recognize Lamort and interrogates the women because they are out after curfew. As they stand there, two soldiers pass by, dragging a dead man wearing a shirt from the old regime. The sight enrages Emilie, who refuses to "see nothing" as Toto demands (Danticat 118). Lamort tries to defuse the situation by saying the password, but Emilie stomps on Toto's foot. In response, Toto aims his rifle at Emilie's head. Lamort screams peace, sees Raymond nearby, and pleads him for help. Raymond tells Toto to let them go, and escorts the women out of the yard. Back on the road, he tells Lamort that the password has changed, and that she should stop saying "peace."

Lamort and Emilie go back to the yellow house. Emilie begins sewing her mother's quilt immediately and Lamort says she has to go home. Emilie begs her to stay, saying that she will give Lamort more money if she stays with her until morning. Lamort says her grandmother will be angry, but agrees to stay. Over the course of the night and the next morning, the two talk about Lamort's mother, named Marie Magdalène, Emilie's mother, named Isabelle, Raymond, and Toto. In the morning before Lamort leaves, Emilie writes down those four names on the back of a photo of her mother and gives it to Lamort, along with some money. She tells Lamort to keep it for posterity.

When Lamort gets home, her grandmother is waiting for her outside. She doesn't move or say anything to Lamort. Lamort speaks first, and tells her grandmother that she wants to be called by her mother's name, Marie Magdalène.

Analysis

The infamously violent and corrupt macoutes who plagued the main characters of "Children of the Sea" and the Haitian populace appear in "The Missing Peace." Previously, the macoutes were only specters of violence and chaos. They seemed to revel in senseless acts of brutality and relish other people's pain. At times, the macoutes appeared inhuman because of these characteristics. Through the story of Lamort, Emilie, Raymond, and Toto, we learn that the macoutes are indeed human beings with emotions. Raymond's relationship with Lamort shows that macoutes can have light-hearted, open relationships with civilians. Intimidation tactics and shows of power aren't necessary in every exchange between macoutes and pedestrian Haitian people. Toto's exchange with Emilie illustrates how many actions of the macoutes are guided by their own insecurities about personal power and the need to be respected. Toto is taken aback and infuriated when Emilie refuses to respect him and obey his orders. His posturing with his rifle is a display meant to put power back into his hands and remind everyone who is in charge. The need to have power, the need to be respected, and the need to be feared are all human traits. Despite their inhumane treatment of others, the macoutes are still people.

The macoutes are not the only foreign presence in "The Missing Peace." Emilie Gallant, a young American in search of her missing journalist mother, brings her own unique flair to the story. With her brash words and initial refusal to back down from Toto's dominance display, Emilie disrupts the placid relationship Lamort had with the macoutes. When she refuses to "see nothing" in the face of the macoutes' brutality, she forces all of the characters to reassess their casual acceptance of death and violence. This exchange does go both ways, however. When Toto shows little-to-no interest in Emilie's American passport, and moves to shoot her despite her American citizenship, Emilie realizes that she has less clout abroad than she thought.

Emilie's presence also adds a new dimension to the theme of mother-daughter relationships in the book. Most of the stories in *Krik? Krak!* feature moments of mothers sacrificing for their daughters–Célianne from "Children of the Sea" and Josephine's grandmother in "Nineteen Thirty-Seven" come to mind. Rarely is this dynamic reversed, as it is in "The Missing Peace." Emilie arrives in Ville Rose and starts asking dangerous questions, thereby putting herself at risk, all for the purpose of discovering what happened to her mother. Despite Lamort's warning about the potential danger of going to the gravesite at night, Emilie still goes, determined to find and retrieve her mother's remains. Emilie's willingness to put herself in danger for the sake of her mother's memory places her in the same category as Josephine from "Nineteen Thirty-Seven": the category of daughters willing to sacrifice for their mothers.

Lamort's relationship with her mother is another key aspect of "This Missing Peace." Lamort's mother died while giving birth to her, a fact that Lamort can never forget because she was named for this tragic event. This constant reminder that she is responsible for her mother's death further complicates Lamort's relationship with a woman she never really met. Lamort's grandmother shapes much of this relationship. She is the one who named Lamort 'death' in the wake of her mother's passing. She is the one who compares Lamort to her mother, telling the young girl that she is as pretty as her mother was. It isn't until the end of the story, when Lamort says she wants to be named Marie Magdalène after her mother, that Lamort assumes control of her relationship with her mother. Rather than be named for her mother's death, Lamort wants to be named in her honor.

Just as there is significance in a name, there is also significance in a title. The title "The Missing Peace" draws on two pivotal plot points from the story. The obvious one is the password Raymond tells Lamort to never forget. 'Peace' is the word that saved Raymond's life in the past and saves Emilie's life in the present. "The Missing" in the title refers to Emilie's missing mother. Not only is Isabella missing from Emilie's life, she is also the missing piece of the quilt-making process. Taken altogether, "The Missing Peace" is about the peace missing from the lives of all story's characters. Lamort sees how quickly her peaceful life and relationship with the macoutes can quickly devolve to violence. Raymond learns that peace with civilians can be hard to preserve. And Emilie lacks inner peace because her questions about her mother's fate cannot be answered or resolved.

Despite the lack of peace, "The Missing Peace" ends on a hopeful note. Lamort has claimed her mother's name and her legacy, and seems determined to forge her own path in the world. Similar to Josephine in "Nineteen Thirty-Seven," Lamort has risen from the ashes of her mother's death and is poised for a new beginning.

Krik? Krak! "Seeing Things Simply" Summary and Analysis

Summary

The story starts with the sounds of a cockfight. The main character, Princesse, has just finished her school day and must pass by the cockfights on her way to her daily appointment. One of the cockfight spectators, an old man, is a former schoolteacher from Port-au-Prince and is rumored to have studied at the Sorbonne in France. As Princesse passes by he tries to make small talk with her, but she brushes him off and continues on her way.

Princesse's daily appointment is with Catherine, a 27-year-old painter from Guadeloupe. As a reward for getting good grades, Princesse's school introduced her to Catherine. Unbeknownst to her school, Princesse has begun modeling for Catherine's nude portraits. It took a while for Princesse to grow comfortable exposing her body, but Catherine has learned how to coax her. As long as no one in Ville Rose sees the portraits, Princesse is okay with being Catherine's subject.

Catherine has Princesse recline on a white cloth, and begins to paint her. The pair talks about a variety of topics, including Catherine's past in France and the art of painting. When Catherine is done painting for the day, she gives Princesse two gourdes and sends her home. By now night has fallen over Ville Rose. The cockfights are over, and a man weeps over the body of his fallen rooster. He begins to bury the rooster, chanting "Ayïbobo" over the grave. The old man from earlier shouts at the man and asks him why he's burying the rooster, when he could be eating it. The other man replies that he is returning the rooster to his fallen father. Just then, the old man catches sight of Princesse and remarks that he is lucky to see her twice in one day. Princesse agrees with him, and hurries on her way.

Princesse goes back to Catherine's house the next day and the day after that for two more painting sessions. During the first of these sessions Catherine has Princesse pose fully clothed on the beach, and the two of them talk about light and how small entities can evoke big changes in the universe. The second session is in Catherine's bedroom, and the discussion is about Catherine's mentor, a French man who died recently. Princesse offers her condolences, but Catherine seems fine.

The following day Princesse visits Catherine again, but Catherine doesn't paint. Rather, they sit and talk on Catherine's veranda. Catherine says she wants to hear Princesse talk, and asks her what color the sky is. Princesse replies that the sky is an indigo blue, like the kind used in laundry. Catherine responds cryptically to Princesse's answer.

The next afternoon when Princesse visits Catherine, the painter is not home. Princesse waits until nightfall for her, walking along the beach and gazing at the ocean. Looking out over the distance, she wishes that she could paint the night skies, the full moon, and the stars. Princesse goes back to Catherine's house again the following day to find that the painter is still missing. This time she walks around Catherine's house three times before going to the beach. On the beach she finds a conch shell and blows into it, creating a "dissonant melody" (Danticat 135). She thinks to herself that she would love to paint the sound created by the shell, and a portrait of herself as a mermaid.

Catherine returns a week later. She had been in Paris, selling her finished portraits and visiting the grave of her mentor. When Princesse arrives at her house, Catherine serves her some iced rum and gives her a portrait as a gift. The painting is of Princesse lying naked on a rock. Princesse is transfixed by the painting, and realizes this is why she wants to make pictures: so that she could leave a piece of herself and the way she observed the world behind when she died.

After visiting with Catherine, Princesse walks home with her portrait. She passes the old man, who says again how lucky he is to see her twice a day. The old man's wife comes along and attempts to drag him home because he is drunk. Princesse watches them for a few moments before sitting in the grass and sketching them in the dust. She finishes their outlines, but leaves their faces blank for someone else to fill in. As she continues home, the sounds of another cockfight pierce the air.

Analysis

"Seeing Things Simply" has a cyclical, repetitious, and slice-of-life feel to it. The cyclical and repetitious feeling of the story can be attributed to a few sources. The first is the fact that the story begins and ends with the sounds of a cockfight. This gives the sense that the story has gone full circle, that it has arrived back at the beginning. The second source is the lack of diversity in the actions of the characters. Day in, day out, Princesse just goes to school and then goes to model for Catherine. She poses, the two women talk, and then Princesse goes home; she wakes up the next day and does it all over again. Catherine, the second main character of the story, also has a repetitive schedule. She waits for Princesse to get out of school, paints the young girl in the afternoon, sends her home, wakes up, and repeats it all over again. The moment that Catherine moves outside of her tightly kept regiment by going to Paris is the only true moment of conflict in the story.

Speaking of conflict, "Seeing Things Simply" has a distinct lack of it, especially when compared to the other stories in *Krik? Krak!* There is no military presence in the story, no mention of the corrupt Haitian government, and no questions about old or new regime. The only physical violence that occurs in the story is between the roosters fighting in the cockfights. Even the lone instance of verbal violence, between the old drunken man and the man with the dead rooster, has a comedic element.

The absence of violence and sweeping, momentous events in "Seeing Things Simply" forces the reader's attention to other aspects of the work, like its use of similes and imagery. One of the first notable similes in the story is the comparison of the cockfight noise to music. This is an apt description of the role the cockfighting itself plays in the overall story. If Princesse, Catherine, and the old man are the stars of the show, then the cockfights are the background music. Another important simile is Princesse likening the sound of a blown conch shell to an SOS call from a distant ship. This figure of speech ties in with the sea and ocean imagery that is scattered throughout "Seeing Things Simply."

This imagery comes alive in Catherine's absence. With her painter friend gone, Princesse pays more attention to the world around her, making observations typical of someone with an artistic eye. She notices how the sky "blends with the sea, stroking the surface the way two people's lips would touch each other's" (Danticat 138). She pays close attention to the feel of the sand and the sound of the ocean as she waits on the beach for Catherine to return. The minute sensory details of the sea and the beach add texture and depth to an otherwise simple story.

"Seeing Things Simply" is a startling departure from the other tales in the *Krik? Krak!* collection. Its lack of violence, different from the other stories, allows for a different side of Haitian life to take center stage–a side not marred by the machinations of a corrupt government or the brutality of an aggressive military force. As we approach the end of the collection, it'll be interesting to see what new directions the remaining stories take us in.

Krik? Krak! "New York Day Women" Summary and Analysis

Summary

Suzette, the narrator of "New York Day Women," is having a typical day in New York City when she sees her strolling through the streets of Manhattan. Suzette is taken aback, because to her knowledge her mother has never been outside of Brooklyn. Her mother has never even seen the office building where Suzette works, and she is also afraid of taking the subway. Shocked and a bit worried, Suzette decides to follow her mother as she walks the streets.

As Suzette tails her mother, her mind is filled with memorable quotes of things her mother has told her in the past. For example, when she sees her mother waiting patiently for cars to pass so she can cross the road, Suzette hears in her head, "In Haiti when you get hit by a car, the owner of the car gets out and kicks you for getting blood on his bumper" (Danticat 144). As her mother walks among the other New Yorkers, Suzette remembers that her mother doesn't even go out to dinner with other people. "If they want to eat with me," Suzette's mother says, "let them come to my house, even if I boil water and give it to them" (Danticat 147).

Suzette is so preoccupied with following her mother that she almost overtakes her. She stops at a wall to rest and watches her mom strut along "as though she owns the sidewalk under her feet" (Danticat 148). Her mother stops to buy a can of soda and to look at a display of African-print dresses. Suzette can tell her mother is thinking about buying her one, and mentally begs her mother not to, because she would just give it to Goodwill. This makes Suzette remember her mother saying, "Why should we give to Goodwill when there are so many people back home who need clothes? We save our clothes for the relatives in Haiti" (Danticat 149).

The next stop is a hot-dog stand, where Suzette's mother buys a frankfurter. Again, Suzette is shocked, because hot dogs are full of salt and her mother always says, "I cannot just swallow salt. Salt is heavier than a hundred bags of shame" (Danticat 149).

The final stop is the park. Suzette's mother walks towards a woman dressed in fitness gear and her young son. The woman gives the child to Suzette's mom and then jogs away. Suzette's mother and the little boy are extremely comfortable with one another. They sit together on a park bench and Suzette's mother gives the child the can of soda she bought earlier. They watch the other kids at the park play while the boy reads a comic book. After an hour passes, the woman returns, her workout completed. Suzette's mother gives the woman her son back and walks further into the park.

By this time, Suzette's one-hour lunch break has ended and she has to hurry back to the office. She takes one last look at her mother before hopping into a taxi. Her mother is standing in the park with other women who are babysitting other people's children. To Suzette, they look like "a Third World Parent-Teacher Association" (Danticat 151).

In the cab, Suzette realizes that her mother never went to any of her Parent-Teacher Association meetings when she was in school. Her mother's accuse for never going was, "You're so good anyway. What are they going to tell me? I don't want to make you ashamed of this day woman. Shame is heavier than a hundred bags of salt" (Danticat 155).

Analysis

Set in New York City, "New York Day Women" is quite literally a departure from the other *Krik? Krak!* stories. Some of our characters have finally been successful in their quest to leave Haitian shores, and have arrived in the heart of America. Or have they really? To Suzette's eyes, while her mother's body might have reached America, her heart and soul never made the trip. Suzette has watched as her mother struggles to come to terms with certain "American" behaviors, like "eating out" and giving to Goodwill. Though these observations are humorous within the context of the story, they are examples of the real and serious struggles immigrants have when arriving in the United States. For so many, culture shock and the difficulty of assimilation are debilitating and make transitioning to America a nearly impossible task.

That is why "New York Day Women" is such a refreshing story to read. After witnessing firsthand her mother's difficulties with American culture, imagine Suzette's shock when she sees that same woman surviving and thriving in the middle of Manhattan. Suzette's mother walks the street confidently "with a happy gait," as if she has lived in New York her entire life (Danticat 143). She interacts easily with vendors and has no problem being with the child she babysits and his mother. At one point of the story, Suzette goes to step in and "save" her mom from an overeager bicycle messenger, only to find that her mother doesn't need saving. It's details like these that make "New York Day Women" not only a comedic story, but also a story of triumph.

Much of "New York Day Women's" humor is derived from the "call and response"-esque format of the story between Suzette and her mother. For example, when Suzette thinks about the exercise bike she wants to buy, she recalls her mother saying, "You are pretty enough to be a stewardess. Only dogs like bones" (Danticat 149). By juxtaposing Suzette's opinions about a topic with quotes from her mother about the same topic, Danticat illuminates the generational gaps that can exist between a mother and her daughter. She also shows the strength of the mother-daughter bond. Despite their disagreements, it is clear that love permeates Suzette's relationship with her mother. This love is revealed in nonlinear ways. Suzette using her entire lunch break to follow her mother around Manhattan, making sure that her mother doesn't need her help, is one example of this love. Suzette's mother refusing to attend Parent-Teacher Association meetings because she doesn't want to embarrass Suzette with her "foreignness" is another example of this love.

As the penultimate story in the *Krik? Krak!* collection, "New York Day Women" is a short and sweet story that transitions us from Haiti to America. Its unique structure allows the reader to view snapshots from the lives of Haitian women in their new environment. However, because of the story's brevity, this view is limited. Perhaps a more complete picture will be offered in the last story.

Krik? Krak! "Caroline's Wedding" Summary and Analysis

Summary

"Caroline's Wedding" begins with Grace, the narrator of the story and Caroline's older sister, calling their mother to share some exciting news. She has just received her American citizenship. Grace's mother, Hermine, is thrilled for her daughter, and instructs her to go right away and apply for a passport. That, according to Hermine, is "truly what's American" (Danticat 156). Grace obeys her mother and goes to the post office to send in the passport application materials. She has to "trade in" her naturalization certificate for a passport application, and without her proof of citizenship she feels "like unclaimed property" (Danticat 156). Ever since Hermine was arrested in a sweatshop raid and placed in immigration jail for three days, Grace's family has "always been very anxious about [their] papers" (Danticat 156).

Back at home, Grace hurries to show her mother the photocopy of her passport application. Hermine says they will celebrate with a pot of her heal-all bone soup. According to Hermine, this soup cures all type of ills. She hopes the soup will succeed in detaching Caroline from her Bahamian finance, Eric. For some reason, Hermine doesn't approve of the match.

Just then, Caroline enters the kitchen. Caroline was born without her left forearm, possibly because the prison doctors gave Hermine a shot of a drug to help her sleep during her three-day incarceration. Seeing that her mother is serving bone soup again, Caroline whispers to Grace that she is getting tired of her mother's constant meddling. Caroline makes a teasing remark to Hermine about the soup. Hermine says that Caroline thinks of herself as so American. At this Grace interjects and tells her sister she's just become a citizen as well. Caroline is already a citizen because she was born on American soil, a fact Grace thinks her sister takes for granted.

Later that night, Grace and Hermine talk in Hermine's bedroom. The discussion is about Caroline's upcoming nuptials, and how much Hermine wishes her daughter would break off the engagement. She wants her daughters to marry nice Haitian men. Talking about marriage reminds Hermine of her own courtship with her now-deceased husband. She shares their story with Grace, and seems to realize for the first time that Caroline will indeed be getting married, whether she approves of the groom or not.

Grace goes back to the room she shares with Caroline to find that her sister is still awake. The sisters sit in the dark and play the free association game Hermine taught them, the same coded call-and-response game Josephine tests Jacqueline with in "Nineteen Thirty-Seven." It is revealed that Hermine is from Ville Rose and was a part of the same secret women's society that Josephine and Défilé were in. Before the girls fall asleep, their mother comes to tell them about a Mass being held at the local church for a dead refugee woman. Grace agrees to go, but Caroline does not.

The ceremony is not heavily attended. There are few other middle-aged women present, in addition to Hermine and Grace. Hermine wears a leather belt around her belly, similar to how old Haitian women wear rags around their torsos when grieving. The priest begins by reciting a list of 129 names, all of them Haitian refugees who died at sea that week. Once he finishes the list, he asks for a special prayer to be said for an unidentified young woman that gave birth on a refugee boat, and who later committed suicide because her baby didn't survive. This woman, of course, is Célianne from "Children of the Sea."

When Hermine and Grace get home, Caroline is still in bed. She asks Grace how Mass was as she continues to pack up her belongings. The packing process has been slow, because Caroline doesn't want to traumatize her mother by moving out immediately. To Hermine's chagrin, Caroline and Eric are not having a big formal wedding in a church, but rather a small civil ceremony. This, along with Eric not officially asking Hermine for permission to marry Caroline, along with a slew of other culture differences, is why Hermine is unhappy about Caroline's wedding.

Changing the subject, Caroline tells Grace that she dreamed of their father last night. Their father died almost ten years ago from untreated prostate cancer, and for the first few months after his death the girls would dream of him nightly. In the dream they would chase after him but never reach him. They never told their mother about these dreams, because she is highly superstitious and reads a lot of symbolism into dreams, the dead, and mourning.

After sharing her dream Caroline pulls out an old photograph of their father. The girls look longingly at the photo. Though ten years have passed since their father's death, they still miss him deeply. Caroline wishes he would send some kind of sign that he approves of her life, her choices, and her fiancé. Caught up in reminiscing, they begin to repeat their father's favorite Haitian proverbs.

Next door, Mrs. Ruiz, the family's Cuban neighbor, is hosting her large extended family for a celebration with blaring rumba music. Caroline and Grace observe the proceedings from a window. Caroline tells Grace that last month Mrs. Ruiz's son was killed trying to hijack a plane in Havana so he could fly it to Miami. The beats of the rumba music remind Grace of their childhood fantasies. In one, Caroline's missing limb would burst out of Hermine's stomach and attach itself to Caroline's stub. They would then go to Mrs. Ruiz's house to celebrate. The girls were always very disappointed when this never happened.

That night, it's Grace's turn to dream of her father. First she dreams that he is at an 18th-century-style masked ball. She tries to run towards him but cannot move. He is standing in a crowd of masked women. Slowly, the women take off their masks, and one of them turns out to be Caroline. Grace wakes up with her face soaked in tears, distraught at the idea of her father and her sister leaving her behind. That morning, she begins writing down a list of her father's crazy escapades and things she learned from him. One of these is a riddle. "Why," Grace's father asked, "is it that when you lose something, it is always in the very last place you look?" "Because," Grace answered, "once you find it, you look no more" (Danticat 167). Another fond memory Grace has of her father is a joke about President for Life Papa Doc Duvalier. These stories and riddles were Grace and Caroline's bedtime stories. As children they didn't fully understand them, but now they are the girls' "sole inheritance" (Danticat 168).

Caroline's wedding is only a month away now. She buys her wedding dress from Goodwill, Hermine decides to wear a pink gown, and Grace will wear a green suit. One night they go over to Eric's house for dinner. As they travel in the taxi, Grace tells Caroline that she wants to throw her a bridal shower. Caroline agrees and gives Grace her address book. It's filled contacts from the school they teach ESL at. This is the same school where Eric and Caroline met. Eric works there as a janitor.

Dinner is a bit awkward. Eric tries his best, but Hermine isn't charmed. He has a learning disability that makes his speech rather slow. Grace plays peacemaker and tells her mother to at least try to eat the food Eric prepared. When Hermine eats very little and just pushes her food around her plate, Grace tells her that she is forbidden to go home and cook later. Caroline goes back home with her sister and mother, but sneaks out when her mother falls asleep, taking a cab back to Eric's. The next morning, Grace covers for her with their mother.

That night, Grace dreams of her father again. This time, he has a voice and calls Grace by her full name, 'Gracina'. Constantly dreaming of her father makes Grace remember moments from their childhood. She remembers how Caroline was nicknamed her parent's "New York child, the child who has never known Haiti," while Grace was their "misery baby," the offspring from the lean years of their lives (Danticat 175). She also recalls how they came to live in New York. Her father got a visa by entering into a fake marriage with a widow leaving Haiti for America. In exchange for some money, the woman took his last name. A few years after arriving stateside, Grace's father divorced the widow and sent for Hermine and Grace.

Before long, the day of Caroline's wedding shower arrives. Besides Grace and Hermine, only four of Caroline's friends attend, along with Mrs. Ruiz. Caroline receives an array of household appliances and a traveling bag for her honeymoon as gifts. Mrs. Ruiz is jovial and lighthearted, promising to deliver Caroline's first child when the time comes. Hermine calls her by her first name, Carmen, and promises to bring her some bone soup. Grace offers her condolences for Mrs. Ruiz's son, to which Mrs. Ruiz responds, "Now why would you want to bring up a thing like that?" (Danticat 183.)

After the guests leave, Caroline packs away her gifts. As she and Grace prepare for bed, Hermine comes bearing one last gift. It's a teddy for Caroline's wedding night. A saleswoman at a department store helped Hermine pick it out. After Caroline goes to bed, Grace goes to her mother's room for one of their chats. They discuss how Hermine and her husband always feared Caroline would settle for someone less than she deserved because of her missing forearm. That's the real reason Hermine doesn't approve of Eric: she thinks Caroline is afraid that no other man will come along.

The night before her wedding, Caroline seems distant. She barely replies to her mother's nagging and acts like she's in another world. At her mother's prodding she tries on her wedding dress one more time, but wears it with a prosthetic arm. Hermine is confused and says that the arm doesn't look very real. Caroline retorts that looking real isn't the point. She has been feeling phantom limb pain, and her doctor believes the stress of the wedding may be the cause. Hermine says if that's true, they should all be experiencing phantom pain.

The day of the wedding, Caroline wakes up looking drowsy and frazzled. She says she woke up feeling as if she doesn't want to get married. Rather than capitalizing on the situation, Hermine comforts her daughter, saying she felt the same way on her wedding day. She and Grace give Caroline a rejuvenating bath, which makes her feel better. Everyone gets ready, with Hermine doing Caroline's makeup and Grace snapping pictures. They pose outside of the courthouse before meeting Eric inside. Grace thinks they look like they're going to a graduation ceremony.

Inside, Eric rushes over to give Caroline a kiss and ogle at her prosthetic arm. Caroline says it's only for the day, but Eric says it suits her fine. Judge Perez, the officiator, is a friend of Eric's. Besides him, the bride, the groom, Hermine, and Grace, no one else is present. Eric's family all live in other states or Cuba. As the ceremony commences, Grace keeps her eyes glued to Caroline's face and watches as her sister slowly begins to fade away. A new, married woman takes her place, and Grace feels as if Caroline is divorcing them for Eric.

The ceremony is over quickly. Grace says she wants to take the newlyweds out for lunch, and Eric replies that their flight to their honeymoon destination leaves at five in the afternoon. Caroline wants to take wedding photos at the Brooklyn Botanic Gardens. Hermine asks why they didn't tell her they were leaving that same night. When they don't answer, she takes her anger out on Grace.

In the end, everyone goes out to lunch at a Haitian restaurant. Hermine doesn't speak, and Caroline doesn't eat. Eric makes a toast, and at her mother's prodding, Grace does too. They go take the wedding photos with a professional photographer, and then go back home to grab Caroline's luggage. The newlyweds say goodbye before taking a taxi the airport. Caroline and Grace sob and Caroline promises to visit when they get back. Later that night, a deliveryman drops off red roses for Hermine. They are from Caroline.

Grace's passport comes in the mail the next day. For the first time, she feels truly secure living in America. She compares it living in a war zone her entire life and finally being given a weapon. She realizes her whole family paid dearly for this piece of paper, and feels like "an indentured servant who had finally been allowed to join the family" (Danticat 214).

The next morning, Grace visits her father's grave in Queens. She brings her passport for him to see, and tells him about Caroline's wedding. She thinks about his funeral, and how she and Caroline wanted to be his pallbearers. Hermine wouldn't let them, saying the thought of young women being pallbearers was too bizarre.

When Grace gets back home, her mom is cooking bone soup. Caroline called, and Hermine takes this as a sign that she misses them. Grace asks if she can drop one bone into the soup pot. Hermine says yes, because it is Grace's soup too. Grace then tries to start the free association game with Hermine, but Hermine wants to ask the first questions. She asks Grace, "Why is it that when you lose something, it is always in the very last place you look?" (Danticat 216.)

Analysis

If "New York Day Women" simply introduces many of the themes and pitfalls of Haitian immigrant life in America, then "Caroline's Wedding" gives us a full treatment of those themes and pitfalls. Generational gaps, the difficulty of assimilating to American culture, questions of national identity…these are all topics that come into play in "Caroline's Wedding." Similar to Suzette and her mother, Grace, Caroline, and Hermine have various differences in opinion. Unlike Suzette and her mother, whose differences were cast in a humorous light, Grace, Caroline, and Hermine all struggle to resolve their disagreements. While Grace seems to bite her tongue and let her mother have her way, Caroline refuses to concede to her mother's opinions and beliefs. Caroline's upcoming wedding to Eric, a Bahamian janitor, is one major subject on which Hermine and her daughters disagree, one that severely strains their mother-daughter relationship. It is only after Hermine accepts that Caroline will indeed be marrying Eric that this strain is eased.

At first, it seems as if Hermine is simply being bigoted when she refuses to approve Caroline's marriage to Eric. In the beginning, all we know is that Hermine wants her daughters to marry Haitian men, and she doesn't like Eric because he is Bahamian. Hermine's discrimination against Eric because of his nationality, while problematic and unjustifiable, is somewhat understandable. Hermine is clearly trying to hold on to the vestiges of her Haitian roots in any way she can. No one in her family has ever married a non-Haitian person, and she wants to keep it that way by mandating whom her daughters can and cannot marry.

The revelation following Eric's dinner party further complicates the situation. Hermine tells Grace that she and her husband always feared that Caroline might settle for someone less than she deserved because of her missing forearm. Because Eric has a speech impediment, Hermine is afraid that he might see himself as settling for Caroline. This, paired with Eric's refusal to follow Haitian nuptial customs (asking for the blessing of the bride's parents, a big wedding in a church, gifts for the bride's mother, etc.) is at the root of Hermine's displeasure over Caroline's wedding.

Hermine's infamous bone soup symbolizes her struggles with her daughters. A cornerstone of Haitian cooking, bone soup is said to cure all sorts of illnesses and right any type of wrong. In the months leading up to Caroline's wedding, Hermine serves bone soup with every dinner meal, hoping that the soup will perform the miracle of breaking up Caroline and Eric. Grace and Caroline eat the soup to placate their mother, but do not believe in its supposed power. In a moment of annoyance, Caroline jokes that she will dunk her entire head into her mother's pot of soup and will blind herself with the scalding liquid. Perhaps then, she reasons, Hermine will realize the soup's ineffectiveness. To Hermine, her daughters' rejection of the bone soup is another sign that they have abandoned their Haitian roots. Half joking, half serious, she laments that her daughters have become American, and makes fun of their lack of taste buds.

Another important symbol in "Caroline's Wedding" is Grace's American passport. When Grace has to trade her naturalization certificate for a passport application at the beginning of the story, she feels like abandoned, unclaimed property. This feeling persists for most of "Caroline's Wedding" and reifies itself in Grace's dreams of her father. In these dreams she can never reach or touch her father, she can only look at him. Caroline, however, stands right next to him in these dreams, and interacts with him. Because Caroline was born on American soil, she was born a citizen and is thus 'claimed property': she is claimed by the American government and claimed by Grace and Caroline's father. Grace never truly feels claimed until her passport arrives in the mail. At that point, she feels "like an indentured servant who finally been allowed to join the family" (Danticat 214). Her passport is like her umbilical cord or a birth certificate—it is her link to her family and proves that she belongs with them.

"Caroline's Wedding" is a fitting end to the *Krik? Krak!* collection. After starting with a failed voyage to the United States in "Children of the Sea," some of our characters have finally made it. But while they left behind some of their problems in Haiti, new problems take their place in America. Successfully leaving Haiti and reaching America is just half the battle. And yet, by ending "Caroline's Wedding" with a peaceful, happy moment between Grace and Hermine, Danticat sends the message that though the United States isn't perfect, it can be home for Haitian immigrants too.

Krik? Krak! Epilogue, "Women Like Us" Summary and Analysis

Summary

The unidentified narrator of "Women Like Us," the epilogue of *Krik? Krak!*, speaks mostly in the second person–that is, in "you" statements. She starts with saying, "you remember thinking while braiding your hair that you look a lot like your mother and her mother before her" (Danticat 217). She then recites the rules of "your mother," foremost among them being that writing is forbidden. It is an indolent act and takes time away from useful hobbies, like learning to cook. There are women who write as they cook, "kitchen poets" who slip phrases into their soups; these women "stuff their daughter's mouths so they say nothing more" (Danticat 218)

In this epilogue, the sound of writing is compared to a "Krik? Krak!" noise, and a notebook is deemed a lonely girl's best confidante. Writing is likened to braiding hair, because when you write you bring together many unruly strands into one unified braid. Some of the strands are long, others short, some thick and heavy, some light and thin. They are like the diverse women in a family, women whose speeches, stories, and sayings slip into a writer's work. Those women don't write down their own stories. They "sit in dark corners and braid their hair in new shapes and twists in order to control the stiffness, the unruliness, the rebelliousness" (Danticat 219).

After this explanation of writing the narrator talks about what happens when the daughter shows her mother her writings for the first time. She describes the mother's disappointment when her daughter explains that writing will be her life's work. For the mother, the sacrifices she made were too great to be repaid with just writing. The narrator then explains the situation from the mother's perspective. Where she's from, writers are tortured and killed if they are men, or called "lying whores," raped, and then killed if they are women. The only people who write where she's from are politicians, and they almost always end up in prison eating their own waste. The mother thinks their family needs a nurse, not a prisoner. She reminds her daughter that there were 999 hardworking women that came before her daughter. 999 women who toiled and sacrificed, and her daughter comes with a ratty notebook? Unacceptable.

And yet, the narrator argues, it was the voices of these women, whispering and murmuring in her head, which pushed the daughter to write in the first place. These 999 women urged her to speak through the tip of her pencil. These 999 women wanted the daughter to tell her mother that women like them do speak, even if it's in a language that's hard to understand. These 999 women form an army around the daughter and are always with her. They boil in her blood and their names roll off of her tongue. And their transcribed stories become the daughter's testament "to the way that these women lived and died and lived again" (Danticat 225).

Analysis

Krik Krak's epilogue isn't so much a story as it is an internal conversation an unidentified woman has with herself. Knowing what we know about Edwidge Danticat's personal history, the most probable narrator of "Women Like Us" is Danticat herself. Like the woman in the epilogue, Danticat also struggled with telling her parents her dreams of being a writer. When the narrator's mother says, "the family needs a nurse," the words sound like something Danticat's own mother could've said to her (Danticat 220). And the woman's determination to continue on writing despite her mother's protestations, because she thinks if she doesn't write the stories "the sky would fall on [her] head" (Danticat 222), sounds like it comes from personal experience.

Though Danticat includes details from her own life in "Women Like Us," she still incorporates the narratives of the fictional women she created in *Krik? Krak!* Célianne, the female letter writer, Josephine, Défilé, Josephine's grandmother, Lili, the night woman, Marie, Lamort, Lamort's grandmother, and the other myriad characters are all present in the epilogue. They are the 999 women who sacrificed and toiled, who made it possible for Danticat to actualize her dream of being a writer. The stories she is telling are theirs, as are the shoulders upon which she stands. With the image of the 999 unified women, Danticat solidifies the linkages she made between her characters in her stories. Like twining strands of hairs together, she unified the voices of these women and created a beautiful braid in the form of *Krik? Krak!*

Krik? Krak! Symbols, Allegory and Motifs

Butterflies (Symbol)

In "Children of the Sea" the female letter writer speaks about the symbolism of butterflies. According to Manman, butterflies can be the carriers of news. Brightly patterned butterflies symbolize happy news, whereas black ones portend death. By the end of the short story, Manman's superstitious beliefs about butterflies appear to have some sliver of truth. Right before the female letter writer learns her sweetheart has died at sea, she sees a black butterfly in the form of her father's hands moving rapidly in the air.

The Madonna Doll (Symbol)

Given to Josephine's great-great-great-grandmother Défilé by her French slave master, the Madonna doll is a porcelain statue of the Virgin Mary. Since Défilé's time, the doll has been passed down the matriarchal line of Josephine's family, from mother to daughter. When Josephine's mother is arrested for witchcraft, she gives the doll to her daughter. The doll becomes Josephine's only remaining tangible connection to her mother. It symbolizes the powerful connection between mothers and daughters.

The Hot Air Balloon (Symbol)

The hot air balloon owned by the Assad family in "A Wall of Fire Rising" plays a central role in the story of Guy, Lili, and Little Guy. Brought to Haiti from America, the hot air balloon is a curiosity, a unique and exciting relic from a place many Haitians dream of fleeing to. Considering America's lure as a place of political freedom and economic opportunity, it is fitting that the hot air balloon symbolizes freedom, hope, and the ability to live life on one's own terms. For Guy, trapped in a life of poverty, the hot air balloon is an obsession. In the end he uses it as his vehicle to escape the chains of his life.

Color (Symbol)

Colors have significance in Haitian culture. In "Caroline's Wedding" the symbolism behind a few colors is explained. Pink represents romance, while green is the color of hope. Finally, red is used to guard widows against their deceased husbands.

Preservation of Innocence (Motif)

The preservation of innocence is an important motif in the short stories of *Krik? Krak!* The most common representation is parents trying to maintain the innocence of their children. In "Night Women," one of the primary concerns of the night woman is ensuring that her son remains ignorant to her life as a sex worker. She concocts fanciful stories about her night activities in the hope of protecting her son's childlike innocence. The night woman doesn't want him introduced to the world of sex before he reaches a certain age; also, she doesn't want her son's perception of her to be altered.

Hermine's behavior in "Caroline's Wedding" is another example of parental preservation of innocence. When her husband dies, Hermine instructs Grace and Caroline to wear red panties to ward off their father. In Haitian folklore the ghosts of dead husbands sometimes come back to lie beside their widows. Sometimes, if their daughter looks a lot like their wife, the husband might mistake one for the other. Thus, mothers and daughters both wear red panties to ward off the dead men and allow their souls to pass along. When she commands her daughters to wear red panties, Hermine is attempting to preserve their sexual innocence.

Krik? Krak! Metaphors and Similes

"i will never go outside again. not even in the yard to breathe the air. they are always watching you, like vultures." (Danticat 5) (Simile)

Here the female narrator of "Children of the Sea" compares the macoutes to vultures. Carrion animals, vultures prey upon weak, dying, or dead organisms for sustenance. They lie in wait for their victims and take advantage of their vulnerability. In their relationship with Haitian citizens, the macoutes are like vultures. Under the Duvalier regime, pedestrian Haitians experienced a lack of civil rights and didn't receive basic services from the Haitian government. This rendered them virtually powerless and susceptible to maltreatment. This empowered the macoutes, and, like vultures, they were able to attack and abuse innocent people in broad daylight without repercussions.

"Maybe the sea is endless. Like my love for you." (Danticat 15) (Simile)

In this simile the male letter writer compares his love for the female letter writer to the sea, claiming that it is as endless as the ocean. In his eyes, his love is as deep, enduring, tranquil, and powerful as the sea.

"Even in a flowered dress, she is lost in a sea of pinstripes and gray suits, high heels and elegant short skirts, Reebok sneakers, dashing from building to building." (Danticat 145) (Metaphor)

In "New York Day Women," Suzette compares the hustle and bustle of Manhattan to the sea because of its fast pace and vastness. Amongst the eclectic mix of New

Yorkers, Suzette's mother is hard to see. This is similar to how objects caught in the foam and waves of the ocean can be hard to see.

"Then like the last burst of lightning out of clearing sky, the boy began." (Danticat 54) (Simile)

As part of a play at his school, Little Guy of "A Wall of Fire Rising" must memorize several monologues. These long speeches are full of revolutionary, incendiary words meant to electrify and galvanize listeners. Thus, it is apt to compare Little Guy's recitation to a bolt of lightning.

Rose (Metaphor)

Rose is the abandoned, dead baby Marie "adopts" in "Between the Pool and the Gardenias." When Marie first sees Rose, the infant is wrapped in a pink blanket and lying on the street next to an open sewer. For Marie, who has experienced several miscarriages, Rose is a gift from God. She compares the baby girl to famous biblical figures like Baby Moses and Baby Jesus.

Krik? Krak! Irony

The Father of the Female Letter Writer (Situational Irony)

The father of the female letter writer in "Children of the Sea" vehemently opposes his daughter's relationship with the male letter writer. Because the young man is from a lower socioeconomic background, the father doubts that he can adequately provide for his daughter. He wants his daughter to marry someone that can improve her already high living standard. Later in the story, we learn that the father of the female letter writer was a gardener from Ville Rose and his wife was from a university-educated family that lived in the city. They also did not have the approval of the mother's family, but got married anyways. Considering how similar his own story is to the female and male letter writers', it is ironic that the father of the female letter writer isn't more understanding and supportive.

Marie's Arrest (Dramatic Irony)

In "Between the Pool and the Gardenias," the story ends with the main character Marie getting arrested. She has been wrongfully accused of killing a baby girl for evil purposes. The person who reports Marie to the authorities is a Dominican man who works with her at the home of a wealthy Haitian couple. Prior to Marie "adopting" Rose, Marie and the Dominican man had been intimate with each other. Because of their shared past, it is logical to think that the Dominican man would be more sympathetic to Marie's situation–at least, more sympathetic than her employers, who already call Marie a "manbo" behind her back. Ironically however, it is the Domincan man, and not Marie's employers, who arranges for her arrest.

Suzette's Mother (Dramatic Irony)

The entire "New York Day Women" story is ironic. From Suzette's mental musings, it seems as if her mother is completely uncomfortable with American customs and the American way of life. According to Suzette, her mother refuses to dine out with other people, she refuses to take the subway, and she rarely steps foot out of the Brooklyn area of the city. So, imagine Suzette's shock when she sees her mother pounding the pavement in the middle of Manhattan. After leaving her mother "at home that morning in her bathrobe, with pieces of newspaper twisted like rollers in her hair," Suzette ironically sees her again in the last place she would have expected (Danticat 144).

Célianne's Identity (Dramatic Irony)

Célianne, the young pregnant girl in "Children of the Sea," makes a posthumous appearance in "Caroline's Wedding": Hermine's church, Saint Agnes Church in New York City, hold a mass in her honor. Ironically, none of the characters in the story knows Célianne's name or her full story. They know nothing about how her baby was conceived, nor do they know the exact circumstances of her death. All they know is that Célianne committed suicide when it became clear her baby was dead. The fact that the reader knows more about Célianne's life than the characters in the story is an example of dramatic irony.

Krik? Krak! Imagery

"White sheets with bright red spots float as our sail. When I got on board I thought I could still smell the semen and the innocence lost to those sheets." (Danticat 2)

The male letter writer from "Children of the Sea" attempts to flee Haiti via a little passenger boat. The sails of the boat are white bed sheets with red stains. Importance is placed on the color of the stains because they suggest the end of someone's virginity. The soiled bed sheets used as sails are an explicit illustration of the loss-of-innocence motif.

The Inmates of Port-au-Prince Prison

Josephine's mother is incarcerated at a prison in Haiti's capital. The living conditions of the prison are dehumanizing. The women prisoners live amongst their waste and are given just enough food to survive. As she paints a desolate picture of prison life, Danticat focuses not on the treatment the women receive, but rather on the effect this treatment has on their bodies. Once robust and voluptuous women have been reduced to "bone-thin women with shorn heads" who carry "clumps of their hair in their bare hands." (Danticat 35) Josephine's mother in particular is a victim of the prison's starvation tactics. So rapid was her weight loss that her extra skin clings "to her bones, falling in layers, flaps, on her face and neck" (Danticat 36).

In addition to starvation, the inmates are also viciously beaten. Again, the reader is not given details of these attacks, but is instead left to read about their aftermath. For example, the teeth of Josephine's mother are stained dark red, "as though caked with blood from the initial beating during her arrest" (Danticat 36). The focus on the result of the maltreatment the prison inmates suffer, rather than on the treatment itself, channels attention to the victims rather than to the victimizers.

The Decomposition of Rose's Body

A few days after Marie "rescues" Rose from the streets of Pétion-Ville, Rose's body begins to decompose rapidly. Danticat describes this process through the use of similes and sensory details. For example, the smell of Rose's body is compared to week-old pig intestines. After four days pass and Rose's skin begins to crack, sink in, and dry up, Marie compares the baby's body to the bodies of her aunts and grandmothers, who have been dead for years. Finally, little details like the flies

Rose's body attracts, the number of times Marie must bathe Rose to keep down the smell of her decaying body, and the way Marie chokes on her breath when she tries to kiss the baby, further help describe how Rose's body decomposes.

Princesse's Imaginary Paintings

After working so closely with Catherine, Princesse longs to create her own paintings. Unlike Catherine's figure-focused works, Princesse's imagined paintings are of somewhat intangible and ephemeral things. Her works depict sounds, textures, and split-second sensations. Princesse's descriptions of her imagined paintings inundate the reader with sensory details and similes. For example, one painting is of "the sound that came out of [a small conch] shell, a moan like a call to a distant ship, an SOS with a dissonant melody" (Danticat 135). Another depicts "the feel of the sand beneath her toes", and another the feeling of cracking empty crab shells between her palms (Danticat 135). By evoking the senses in her descriptions of Princesse's paintings, Danticat allows the reader to visualize those imagined pieces of art.

Krik? Krak! A Timeline of Haitian History

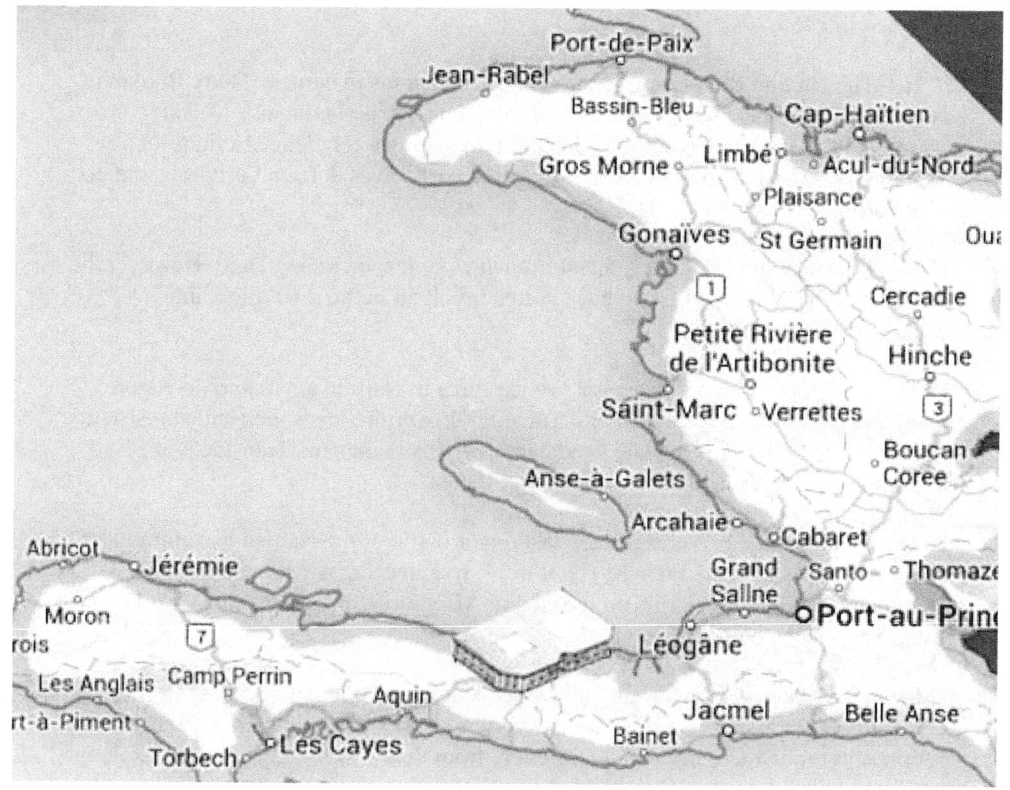

Set mostly in the island nation of Haiti, *Krik? Krak!* is heavily influenced by the tumultuous political and social history of the small Caribbean republic. Some events of Haiti's history are only subliminally alluded to, while others, like the massacre of Haitians living in the Dominican Republic, are explicitly referenced. Not only does Haiti's history deeply impact the events of the book, it also affects the lives and decisions of *Krik? Krak!*'s characters. Therefore, a general knowledge of Haitian history would greatly increase a reader's understanding and overall appreciation of the work. To that end, a timeline of key events in Haitian history is provided below.

1492—Christopher Columbus discovers the island of Hispaniola, which present-day Haiti shares with the Dominican Republic. He founds the first Spanish community near Cap-Haïtien, on the north coast of Haiti.

1503—The first African slaves are brought to Hispaniola for forced labor.

1665—French settlers found Port-au-Prince on the northwest coast of Hispaniola. The French name their half of the island "Saint-Dominique" and authorize the slave trade within it.

1751—François Mackandal, a Haitian Maroon leader in Saint-Dominique, leads slave rebellions in the northern part of the country. Mackandal is later captured and executed in 1758.

1791—The Haitian Revolution for emancipation begins in earnest. Dutty Boukman, a slave who became a leader in the revolution, and Cécile Fatiman, a Vodou priestess, lead a Vodou ceremony where hundreds of slaves pledge to fight for freedom. A few days after the ceremony, a force of slaves defeats European soldiers near Port-au-Prince.

1794—France abolishes slavery in all French colonies, including Haiti. However, by this time both Spain and Britain have gotten involved in the revolution, thus complicating the situation.

1802—Napoleon Bonaparte sends a French force to Haiti in an attempt to restore French rule. Haitian military general Toussaint Loverture leads the Haitian resistance against the French but is defeated and captured. His lieutenant, Jean-Jacques Dessalines, assumes leadership of the rebel forces.

1803—At the Battle of Vertiéres, the last major battle of the Haitian Revolution, Haitian forces defeat the French. The Europeans surrender at Môle Saint-Nicolas, effectively ending French rule on the island. Also during this year the flag of Haiti is created and sewn by Catherine Fion.

1804—Dessalines declares Haiti an independent nation and names himself Governor-General. He also orders the massacre of any remaining white French people and French-Creoles. White deserters from the French army are spared, along with a group of doctors and professionals.

1806—Dessalines is assassinated and Henri Christophe is appointed president for four years.

1807—Haiti is divided into the northern State of Haiti and the southern Republic of Haiti. Each country has its own government and president, with Christophe president of the state and Alexandre Pétion president of the republic.

1820—Following the suicide of Henri Christophe, Haiti is reunited under Jean-Pierre Boyer, the then-president of the republic.

1825—In exchange for recognizing Haiti's independence, King Charles X of France imposes a 150 million franc (today, 40 billion US dollars) indemnity on the Haitian government. This amount is later reduced to 90 million franc, which the Haitians finish paying in 1879.

1843-1878—Haiti experiences a period of immense political disarray and upheaval. It sees 10 different presidencies and 1 monarchy. Also during this time the United States recognizes Haiti as a sovereign state and the Dominican Republic declares its independence from Haiti.

1879—Lysius Salomon is elected as President of Haiti. He institutes many reforms and pays off Haiti's remaining debt to France.

1904—Haiti celebrates 100 years of independence.

1915—The United States' 19 year-occupation of Haiti begins with the arrival of 3,000 U.S. Marines in Port-au-Prince.

1929—Haiti and the Dominican Republic sign a treaty establishing the border between the two countries.

1934—The last US forces withdraw from Haiti, ending the US occupation.

1937—The Dominican armed forces, under the orders of Dominican President Rafael Trujillo, massacre between 20-35 thousand Haitian people living in the Dominican Republic.

1957—Dr. François "Papa Doc" Duvalier is elected President of Haiti. He runs on a populist and Black Nationalist platform and uses his rural militia, the Tonton Macoute, to defend his rule. During his regime 30-60 thousand Haitians were murdered, and many more fled to the United States.

1964—President Duvalier is named President for Life of Haiti.

1971—The National Assembly of Haiti allows Duvalier to name his son, Jean-Claude "Baby Doc" Duvalier, as his successor. Later this year Papa Doc dies and Baby Doc ascends to the presidency.

1986—Baby Doc flees Haiti and exiles himself in France.

1987—Voters are massacred at the presidential election to replace Baby Doc. The election is rescheduled, but approximately 96 percent of voters boycott it.

1990—Jean Bertrand Aristide, famous in Haiti for his support of the poor, becomes the first democratically elected President of Haiti with 68% of the popular vote.

1991—A military coup forces President Aristide into exile. Thousands of Haitians begin to flee the country again via boat. Those that are not sent back to Haiti by the US government settle in South Florida.

1994—The military government resigns at the behest of the U.S. government and Aristide returns as President.

2004—Haiti celebrates 200 years of independence. Former Haitian soldiers carry out guerilla attacks and capture the country's 2nd largest city. Aristide resigns from office and flees from Haiti. Later he will claim that he was forced to resign by the U.S. government.

2006—René Preval is elected president in an election U.N. peacekeepers oversee.

2010—A 7.0 magnitude earthquake strikes Haiti, killing up to 316 thousands and leaving 1.6 million homeless. The country has yet to fully recover from the disaster.

2011—Michael Martelly is elected President of Haiti.

2016—President Martelly steps down as president. A provisional government led by Prime Minister Evans Paul is left in control of the country until an interim president is chosen.

Krik? Krak! Literary Elements

Genre

Short Story; Realistic Fiction; Historical Fiction; Coming of Age

Setting and Context

The stories of Krik? Krak! are set in New York City and in various locations around Haiti, a island nation in the Caribbean. The context is the totalitarian regimes of the Duvaliers.

Narrator and Point of View

Some stories in Krik? Krak! are told in the first person while others are told in the third person omniscient narrative perspective.

Tone and Mood

Slice of Life; Mystical; Tragic; Revolutionary

Protagonist and Antagonist

The protagonists of Krik? Krak! are predominately the female main characters in each story. The lone exceptions are the male letter writer in "Children of the Sea" and Guy in "A Wall of Fire Rising." The minor antagonists change with each story, but the overarching villain is the corrupt Duvalier government that oppresses the Haitian people.

Major Conflict

The major conflict of each story is different. A description of each is below:

"Children of the Sea"—The male letter writer must flee Haiti to save his life while his lover remains behind and tries to carve out an existence under an oppressive government.

"Nineteen Thirty-Seven"—Jacqueline struggles to come to terms with her mother's imprisonment and probable death.

"A Wall of Fire Rising"—Guy tries to carve out a livelihood for his wife and son in spite of the lack of economic opportunities and his own crushing depression.

"Night Women"—The night woman tries to provide a living for her son while maintaining his innocence.

"Between the Pool and the Gardenias"—Marie, after suffering several miscarriages, rescues a dead baby from the city streets and struggles to keep it a secret.

"The Missing Peace"—Lamort is drafted to help Emilie uncover the truth of her mother's death, while dodging the violence of the macoutes.

"Seeing Things Simply"—Princesse models for a French painter and in the process must discover her own sense of self.

"New York Day Women"—Suzette follows her mother around New York City and struggles to reconcile this version of her mother with the version she has always known.

"Caroline's Wedding"—Caroline is getting married and her sister and mother need to find a new equilibrium for their lives.

Climax

The climax of each story is different. A description of each is below:

"Children of the Sea"—The male letter writer throws overboard the journal he using to pen his letters to his lover.

"Nineteen Thirty-Seven"—Josephine's mother dies.

"A Wall of Fire Rising"—Guy steals the hot air balloon and commits suicide.

"Night Women"—The night woman sleeps with Emmanuel.

"Between the Pool and the Gardenias"—The Dominican gardener catches Marie with Rose and reports her to the gendarmes.

"The Missing Peace"— Toto almost shoots Emilie.

"Seeing Things Simply"—Catherine disappears.

"New York Day Women"—Suzette's mother meets with the little boy she babysits and his mother.

"Caroline's Wedding"—The day of Caroline's wedding.

Foreshadowing

When the female letter writer thanks her father for saving her life, he waves his hand back and forth to signify that he doesn't need her gratitude. In this moment, his rapidly moving hand resembles a black butterfly. Black butterflies symbolize death, and this one foreshadows the male letter writer's passing. The female letter writer tries to run away from the bad omen, but it is too late. Her lover has already drowned in the sea.

Understatement

N/A.

Allusions

In Krik? Krak! there are numerous historical references to Haiti's political turmoil. The dictatorships of François Duvalier and his son are the backdrop for the stories in the collection. They have an indelible impact on characters and events of the stories. Other historical allusions include a reference to Haiti's rocky relationship with the Dominican Republic and the United States' nineteen-year occupation of Haiti.

In addition to historical references there are also a plethora of religious allusions to Voudou and Christianity. These allusions are sprinkled throughout the collection but are concentrated in "Nineteen Thirty-Seven." Finally, in "Caroline's Wedding," Hermine references Pelé, the famous Brazilian soccer player.

Imagery

See "Imagery" section of the guide.

Paradox

The letter writers in "Children of the Sea" have very distinct styles. The male letter writer has perfect grammar and writes in a somewhat formal, gentile style. The female letter writer cares significantly less about grammatical correctness and eschews the rules of capitalization. This is a bit paradoxical, considering that the male letter writer is of a lower socioeconomic background than the woman and presumably had less of an education.

Parallelism

In "Nineteen Thirty-Seven," Jacqueline wears a piece of black cloth around her stomach to mourn Défilé. This parallels what Hermine does in "Caroline's Wedding" to grieve for Célianne, the pregnant woman in "Children of the Sea."

Metonymy and Synecdoche

N/A.

Personification

"There was a point in the far distance where the sky almost seemed to blend with the sea, stroking the surface the way two people's lips would touch each other's" (Danticat 133).

In this excerpt, the sky and sea are given the characteristics of two lovers.

Krik? Krak! Links

Poto Mitan: Haitian Women Pillars of the Global Economy

http://potomitan.net

The official website of *Poto Mitan: Haitian Women Pillars of the Global Economy,* a film written and narrated by Edwidge Danticat.

A Conversation with Edwidge Danticat

https://web.archive.org/web/20081104091003/http://www.randomhouse.com/vintage/danticat.html

An interview with Edwidge Danticat conducted by Behind the Books, a literacy nonprofit based in New York City.

Krik? Krak! Essay Questions

1. **In "Children of the Sea," the names of the two lovers are never revealed to the reader. Why do you think this is?**

   Danticat's refusal to tell us the names of "Children of the Sea's" main characters is a purposeful and calculated move. At first, the missing names confuse the reader and make it difficult to conceptualize the characters. As the tale progresses, however, the plot of the story and the suffering of the characters take center stage, rendering the absent names a minor issue. What matters isn't *who* the characters are, but *what* they endure. Their identities aren't as important as the trials and tribulations they face.

   In addition, by not assigning the tragic, star-crossed lovers of "Children of the Sea" names, Danticat gives their story a sense of universality. They could be any number of Haitian couples torn apart by the corrupt Duvalier government. Even more broadly, they could be any couple that has ever been torn apart by war and/or an unstable government.

2. **Compare and contrast Grace's relationship with Hermine and Caroline's relationship with Hermine.**

   Grace is nicknamed her mother and father's "misery baby" while Caroline is their "child of the promised land." This is because Grace was their offspring from their lean, struggling days in Haiti, while Caroline was born in America during their more financially secure days. These distinctions between the girls definitely impact their respective relationships to their mother. Until she gets her citizenship and American passport, Grace feels as if she's not a real member of her family. As such, she's less likely to challenge her mother or go against her wishes, because she fears being abandoned. While Caroline refuses to take part in certain "Haitian" customs, like going to Mass to mourn Haitian refugees who are strangers to her, Grace always accompanies her mother to these events. Because her citizenship was never in question, Caroline doesn't feel the same pressures as Grace. She feels secure in her place in their family, and so she doesn't harbor the same fear of abandonment that her older sister does. That is why she feels more comfortable forging her own path against her mother's wishes.

3. **Analyze the role of national and international politics in the stories presented in *Krik? Krak!***

   The impact of domestic and international politics on the *Krik? Krak!* stories cannot be overstated. The corrupt regimes of Haiti's many presidents, most notably the Duvaliers, clearly play an influential role in the lives and decisions of the characters. In "Children of the Sea," one of the main characters attempts to flee those regimes and loses his life in the process. In "A Wall of Fire Rising," the lives of Guy, Little Guy, and Lili are unequivocally changed because of Haiti's lack of economic opportunities for its citizens. And despite their love for their mother country, Suzette's mother and Hermine (from "New York Day Women" and "Caroline's Wedding" respectively) decide to leave their beloved Haiti, because its tumultuous politics make it difficult to raise their daughters there.

International politics also play a commanding role in the *Krik? Krak!* collection. The most notable example is the 1937 massacre of Haitians living in the Dominican Republic. This genocidal event, ordered by the Dominican president at the time Rafael Trujillo, is the inspiration for the story "Nineteen Thirty-Seven." This horrific event left scars on Josephine and her mother, and helped forge strong matrilineal bonds in their family for generations to come. And as the most common destination for emigrating Haitians, the United States is also an important country in *Krik? Krak!* The nearness of the United States and its history of intervention in Haiti and its affairs make it a logical choice for Haitians seeking economic opportunities and political freedom.

4. **Discuss gender *vis-à-vis* personal and political power in Haiti as they are presented in *Krik? Krak!***

   There are few instances in *Krik? Krak!* where it is obvious that a character's gender impacts their power in a situation. The first of these involves the parent's of the female letter writer from "Children of the Sea." When the macoutes are beating Madan Roger, the letter writer's mother wants to run to her aid, but her husband physically stops her. He decides for the whole family that they will not intervene in the situation, because he is afraid of putting a target on their backs. In this scenario, a man usurps and undermines a women's personal power and autonomy over her own actions.

   Another example of the discrepancies between male and female power in Haiti comes from "Between the Pool and the Gardenias." The Dominican man is able to get the gendarmes to investigate Marie on his word alone. Though he is a foreigner, in the game of he-said/she-said, he wins. While Rose's dead body does not help the situation, Marie will most likely not be given a chance to explain herself. The tendency in Haiti to automatically condemn any woman accused of being a witch seals her fate.

5. **Analyze this quote from "Night Women." What literary elements does Danticat use in the quote? Which themes or motifs does the quote draw upon, and how are they used?**

   > **Shadows shrink and spread over the lace curtain as my son slips into bed. I watch as he stretches from a little boy into**

> **the broom-size of a man, his height mounting the innocent fabric that splits our one-room house into two spaces, two mats, two worlds (Danticat 81).**

Rich in imagery, this excerpt from "Night Women" includes examples of metaphors and anthropomorphism. The son of the night woman is compared to a broom, while his shadow is anthropomorphized and changes shape like a contorting body. The son's transformation from a boy to a man evokes the loss-of-innocence motif, and the "innocent fabric" that splits the night woman's house into "two spaces, two mats, two worlds," adds a sense of the mystic to the quote.

Krik? Krak! Quizzes

1. **What is the name of Josephine's mother in "Nineteen Thirty-Seven?"**
   A. Hermine
   B. Jacqueline
   C. Her name is not given
   D. Défilé

2. **Which animal does the male letter writer compare his lover to?**
   A. A vulture
   B. A snail
   C. A dolphin
   D. A butterfly

3. **What do bright butterflies symbolize?**
   A. Freedom
   B. Beauty
   C. Love
   D. Happy news

4. **Why is the male letter glad there are no children on the boat?**
   A. Because he thinks a boat is no place for a child
   B. Because they would remind him of the hopelessness of the future in Haiti
   C. Because they would cry all day long
   D. Because there wouldn't be enough food to feed them

5. **Where is the boat's final destination?**
   A. Key West, Florida
   B. Miami, Florida
   C. Havana, Cuba
   D. Santa Domingo, Dominican Republic

6. **Which faith is highly represented on the boat?**
   A. Voudou
   B. Protestantism
   C. Islam
   D. Catholicism

7. **What does the female letter writer wish for?**
   A. A plane ticket to America
   B. Wanga magic
   C. An end to the Duvalier regime
   D. The return of her lover

8. **The following excerpt is an example of which literary element: "they are always watching you, like vultures"**

   A. Personification
   B. Simile
   C. Symbolism
   D. Metaphor

9. **Which of the following is NOT a word the father of the female letter writer uses to describe his daughter?**

   A. Man-crazy
   B. Whore
   C. Selfish
   D. Pig peasant

10. **What is the name of Haiti's currency?**

    A. Peso
    B. Reale
    C. Dollar
    D. Gourde

11. **What nickname is given to the friends of the male letter writer?**

    A. The youth feds
    B. The macoutes
    C. The young revolutionaries
    D. The radio six

12. **Which of the following does NOT describe Madan Roger?**

    A. She is brutally beaten by the macoutes
    B. She carries the head of her dead son through the streets of Port-au-Prince
    C. She is the neighbor of the male letter writer's family
    D. She is the mother of a slain youth federation member

13. **To where does the family of the female letter writer hope to escape?**

    A. the Dominican Republic
    B. Pétionville
    C. Port-au-Prince
    D. Ville Rose

14. **Which theme does the possible return of the old president represent?**

    A. Hope
    B. Freedom
    C. Brutality
    D. National Identity

15. **How does the father of the female letter writer protect his daughter?**
    A. He bribes the macoutes
    B. He sends away the male letter writer
    C. He plans to relocate the family to Pétionville
    D. He arranges for her to marry a soldier

16. **What do they name Célianne's baby?**
    A. Swiss
    B. Star
    C. Sun
    D. Soleil

17. **Which literary element does the following quote BEST represent? "Think of it. They are fighting about being superior when we all might drown like straw"**
    A. Simile
    B. Hyperbole
    C. Irony
    D. Anthropomorphism

18. **What is the name of Célianne's brother?**
    A. Lionel
    B. Guy
    C. Konpé
    D. Raymond

19. **How old is Célianne?**
    A. 19
    B. 16
    C. 18
    D. 15

20. **Which of the following is NOT something Ville Rose is known for?**
    A. Pink colored houses
    B. Coffee
    C. Painters and poets
    D. Yellow cows

21. **What does Josephine buy for her mother to eat?**
    A. Fried pork and plantains
    B. Fried pork and cabbage
    C. Fried chicken and cabbage
    D. Fried chicken and plantains

22. **Which of the following is NOT a major theme of "Nineteen Thirty-Seven?"**

A. Mysticism
B. Hope
C. National Identity
D. Mother-daughter relationships

23. **Why was Josephine's mother arrested?**

A. Because at night she sprouts wings of flames
B. Because she killed her friend's baby
C. Because she tried to illegally immigrate to the Dominican Republic
D. Because she is believed to be a witch

24. **What does the Madonna doll symbolize?**

A. The role of mysticism in Haiti
B. The connection between the women of Josephine's family
C. Haiti's rocky history with the Dominican Republic
D. The love between Josephine's great-great-great grandmother and her husband

25. **What do Josephine and her mother wear when they go to the Massacre River?**

A. White sashes
B. Black sashes
C. Black dresses
D. White dresses

Quiz 1 Answer Key

1. **(D)** Défilé
2. **(B)** A snail
3. **(D)** Happy news
4. **(B)** Because they would remind him of the hopelessness of the future in Haiti
5. **(B)** Miami, Florida
6. **(B)** Protestantism
7. **(B)** Wanga magic
8. **(B)** Simile
9. **(D)** Pig peasant
10. **(D)** Gourde
11. **(D)** The radio six
12. **(C)** She is the neighbor of the male letter writer's family
13. **(D)** Ville Rose
14. **(A)** Hope
15. **(A)** He bribes the macoutes
16. **(A)** Swiss
17. **(C)** Irony
18. **(A)** Lionel
19. **(D)** 15
20. **(A)** Pink colored houses
21. **(A)** Fried pork and plantains
22. **(B)** Hope
23. **(D)** Because she is believed to be a witch
24. **(B)** The connection between the women of Josephine's family
25. **(D)** White dresses

Krik? Krak! Quizzes

1. **Who is Jacqueline?**
   A. Another inmate at the prison
   B. A friend of Josephine's
   C. Another woman that also went to the Massacre River
   D. The friend that accused Défilé of killing her baby

2. **Which of the following is NOT a major theme of "Children of the Sea?"**
   A. Brutality
   B. Hope
   C. Mother-daughter relationships
   D. Love

3. **Why does the old man on the boat hope to be mistaken for Cuban?**
   A. The U.S. government is biased against Haitians
   B. He is worried that negative stereotypes about Haitian people turn the immigration officers against them
   C. He wants the Coast Guard to take them to Cuba
   D. The Coast Guard is more likely to take them to America if they are Cubans

4. **Which is NOT a detail from the male letter writer's dream about heaven?**
   A. There were mermaids dancing and singing in Latin
   B. The female letter writer was there with her family
   C. There were sharks and mermaids all around him
   D. When he tried to speak, only bubbles came out of his mouth

5. **What is the name of the Dominican leader that led the 1937 massacre?**
   A. Jacinto Peynado
   B. Manuel Troncoso
   C. Dios Trujillo
   D. Rafael Ureña

6. **How does Josephine's mother die?**
   A. The disease she contracted in the prison killed her
   B. The prison guards beat her to death
   C. She was shot as she tried to escape from the prison
   D. She died from the injuries she sustained during her arrest

7. **What do Défilé's prison mates do to honor her?**
    A. They build a cross for her in their cell
    B. They give Josephine all of her mother's belongings
    C. They hold a nighttime vigil
    D. They murder the prison guard that killed her

8. **Who is the famous Haitian figure alluded to in "A Wall of Fire Rising"?**
    A. Dutty Boukman
    B. Cécile Fatiman
    C. Toussaint L'Overture
    D. Georges Biassou

9. **What is Little Guy's nickname at school?**
    A. Pepper head
    B. Guy Jr.
    C. Corn head
    D. Boukman

10. **What two things does the hot air balloon symbolize?**
    A. Freedom and Bigotry
    B. Freedom and Hopelessness
    C. Freedom and Exclusivity
    D. Hopelessness and Economic Prosperity

11. **What is Little Guy compared to when he is performing the play?**
    A. Thunder
    B. Boukman
    C. Lightning
    D. A wall of fire

12. **Who installed the large television near the sugar mill?**
    A. The macoutes
    B. The Assads
    C. The gendarmes
    D. The government

13. **Which are the main themes of "A Wall of Fire Rising"?**
    A. Freedom and Hope
    B. Hope and Love
    C. Hope and Brutality
    D. Freedom and Love

14. **Where was Guy born?**
    A. In the same shanty house he currently lives in
    B. At his family's home in Ville Rose
    C. In the shadow of the sugar mill
    D. At a hospital in Port-au-Prince

15. **Why is Guy obsessed with the hot air balloon?**

A. He once wanted to be an engineer and is fascinated by the technology

B. He wants to use it to fly away

C. He hopes to get a job flying it for the Assads

D. He wants to sell it and use the money to support his family

16. **Little Guy's play has many passionate lines. Which of the following is most impacted by those lines?**

A. The story's tone

B. The story's characters

C. The story's plot

D. The story's atmosphere

17. **Which person has the biggest impact on Guy's decision to commit suicide?**

A. Lili

B. Little Guy

C. Guy's father

D. Young Assad

18. **Who tells Lili that Guy stole the hot air balloon?**

A. A woman from the market

B. Little Guy

C. A sugar mill worker

D. Young Assad

19. **Why does Lili choose to keep Guy's eyes open once he has been pronounced dead?**

A. Because she wants to look into her husband's eyes

B. Because she doesn't want anyone to touch Guy's body

C. Because Guy always liked to look at the sky

D. Because she wants Little Guy to see his father's eyes one last time

20. **What does the night woman's red scarf symbolize?**

A. Loss of innocence

B. The death of her husband

C. Her life as a sex worker

D. Her son's ignorance

21. **What does Emmanuel call the night woman?**

A. A waterfall

B. A storm

C. A hurricane

D. A tornado

22. **Which of these is the main theme in "Night Women?"**
    A. Love
    B. Loss of innocence
    C. Hope
    D. Mysticism

23. **The following quote is an example of what literary element? "Shadows shrink and spread over the lace curtain as my son slips into bed."**
    A. Metaphor
    B. Simile
    C. Anthropomorphism
    D. Personification

24. **Which is NOT a word the night woman uses to describe her son?**
    A. Lover
    B. Star
    C. Butterfly
    D. Broom-like

25. **What type of flowers does Emmanuel bring for the night woman?**
    A. Tulips
    B. Bougainvillea
    C. Daisies
    D. Roses

Quiz 2 Answer Key

1. **(C)** Another woman that also went to the Massacre River
2. **(C)** Mother-daughter relationships
3. **(D)** The Coast Guard is more likely to take them to America if they are Cubans
4. **(C)** There were sharks and mermaids all around him
5. **(C)** Dios Trujillo
6. **(B)** The prison guards beat her to death
7. **(A)** They build a cross for her in their cell
8. **(A)** Dutty Boukman
9. **(A)** Pepper head
10. **(C)** Freedom and Exclusivity
11. **(C)** Lightning
12. **(D)** The government
13. **(A)** Freedom and Hope
14. **(C)** In the shadow of the sugar mill
15. **(B)** He wants to use it to fly away
16. **(D)** The story's atmosphere
17. **(C)** Guy's father
18. **(B)** Little Guy
19. **(C)** Because Guy always liked to look at the sky
20. **(C)** Her life as a sex worker
21. **(A)** A waterfall
22. **(A)** Love
23. **(C)** Anthropomorphism
24. **(B)** Star
25. **(B)** Bougainvillea

Krik? Krak! Quizzes

1. **Who reports Marie to the gendarmes?**
   A. Her husband
   B. The Dominican man
   C. Monsieuer
   D. Madame

2. **Which is NOT a name Marie wanted to give her unborn children?**
   A. Célianne
   B. Josephine
   C. Jacqueline
   D. Défilé

3. **Where does Marie live?**
   A. Pétionville
   B. Port-au-Prince
   C. Cap-Haïtien
   D. Ville Rose

4. **Which of the following is NOT a literary device used in "Between the Pool and the Gardenias?"**
   A. Metaphor
   B. Personification
   C. Simile
   D. Parallelism

5. **Marie compares Rose to each of the following EXCEPT:**
   A. An angel
   B. Pig intestines
   C. Baby Moses
   D. An African doll

6. **What is the major theme of "Between the Pool and the Gardenias?"**
   A. Brutality
   B. Mysticism
   C. Love
   D. National Identity

7. **Madame and Monsieur think Marie might be a:**
   A. Manbo
   B. Mancoute
   C. Houngan
   D. Lougarou

8. **Why does Marie try to keep Rose a secret?**
   A. Because she knows outside of Port-au-Prince people are more superstitious
   B. Because she is afraid the authorities will take Rose away from her
   C. Because she wants to keep Rose as a surprise for her husband
   D. Because she doesn't want to share Rose

9. **Who does NOT visit Marie in her dreams?**
   A. Eveline
   B. Lili
   C. Défilé
   D. Célianne

10. **According to Madame and Monsieur, what is "holding Haitians back?"**
    A. Their belief in Voudou
    B. Their pride
    C. Their corrupt presidents
    D. Their violence

11. **What does Marie compare herself to?**
    A. A biblical mother
    B. An abandoned baby
    C. A dirty piece of paper
    D. Spoiled goods

12. **The following quote BEST represents which literary element? "It seemed like she had aged in four days as many years as there were between me and my dead aunts and grandmothers."**
    A. Parallelism
    B. Hyperbole
    C. Metaphor
    D. Simile

13. **Why does Marie finally decide to bury Rose?**
    A. Because she feels guilty about not putting Rose'
    B. Because she fears her employers will discover Rose's body
    C. Because Rose's body begins to attract flies
    D. Because she wants to complete her ritual with Rose's body

14. **The following quote is an example of which literary element? "He closed his eyes as though the details were never any farther than a stage behind his eyelids."**
    A. Characterization
    B. Simile
    C. Metaphor
    D. Setting

15. **Why does Toto shoot Raymond?**
   A. Because he isn't sure if Raymond is old or new regime
   B. Because he is secretly a spy for the old regime
   C. Because he is jealous of Raymond's relationship with Lamort
   D. Because he wants to take Raymond's place in the military

16. **What is the climax of "Between the Pool and the Gardenias?"**
   A. When Marie's employers call her a manbo
   B. When Marie finds Rose in the streets
   C. When the Dominican calls the gendarmes
   D. When the Dominican catches Marie burying Rose

17. **Where does Toto shoot Raymond?**
   A. In the leg
   B. In the arm
   C. In the torso
   D. In the shoulder

18. **What is the password of the macoutes?**
   A. Corruption
   B. Duvalier
   C. Papa Doc
   D. Peace

19. **What is the climax of "The Missing Peace?"**
   A. When Toto almost shoots Emilie
   B. When Toto shoots Raymond
   C. When Raymond answers Lamort's plea for help
   D. When Toto catches Lamort and Emilie at the gravesite

20. **How did Lamort's mother die?**
   A. She died while fleeing to Miami
   B. She was killed in Ville Rose for being old regime
   C. She died in the coup in Port-au-Prince
   D. She died giving birth to Lamort

21. **What is Emilie's last name?**
   A. Gallant
   B. Gerard
   C. Giovanni
   D. Guten

22. **What is the main theme of "The Missing Peace?"**
   A. Love
   B. National Identity
   C. Mother-daughter relationships
   D. Hope

23. **Where is Catherine from?**

A. France
B. Haiti
C. Guadeloupe
D. The United States

24. **Princesse wants to paint all of the following EXCEPT:**

A. The sunset over the ocean
B. The night sky
C. The sound of a conch shell
D. The feel of the sand beneath her toes

25. **How old is Princesse?**

A. 18
B. 17
C. 16
D. 15

Quiz 3 Answer Key

1. **(B)** The Dominican man
2. **(D)** Défilé
3. **(A)** Pétionville
4. **(B)** Personification
5. **(A)** An angel
6. **(B)** Mysticism
7. **(A)** Manbo
8. **(A)** Because she knows outside of Port-au-Prince people are more superstitious
9. **(D)** Célianne
10. **(A)** Their belief in Voudou
11. **(C)** A dirty piece of paper
12. **(D)** Simile
13. **(C)** Because Rose's body begins to attract flies
14. **(B)** Simile
15. **(A)** Because he isn't sure if Raymond is old or new regime
16. **(D)** When the Dominican catches Marie burying Rose
17. **(A)** In the leg
18. **(D)** Peace
19. **(A)** When Toto almost shoots Emilie
20. **(D)** She died giving birth to Lamort
21. **(A)** Gallant
22. **(C)** Mother-daughter relationships
23. **(C)** Guadeloupe
24. **(A)** The sunset over the ocean
25. **(C)** 16

Krik? Krak! Quizzes

1. **Why does Princesse want to paint?**
   A. Because she wants to use the art world to escape from Haiti
   B. Because she wants to experience the prestige and lifestyle that comes with being an artist
   C. Because she wants to leave her perspective of the world behind when she dies
   D. Because she wants to be like her idol Catherine

2. **How does "Seeing Things Simply" end?**
   A. Catherine finally returns
   B. The way it began
   C. The old man dies
   D. Princesse creates her first painting

3. **What does Suzette's mother compare shame to?**
   A. Drowning
   B. Quicksand
   C. Poupou
   D. Salt

4. **Which is NOT a quote from Suzette's mother?**
   A. "Oh no, he doesn't kiss me that way anymore."
   B. "What has this world come to when the sun can no longer warm God's creatures?"
   C. "Many graves to kiss when I go back. Many graves to kiss."
   D. "You are pretty enough to be a stewardess. Only dogs like bones."

5. **What does Suzette's mother buy for the young boy she babysits?**
   A. A soda
   B. A comic book
   C. A t-shirt
   D. A hot dog

6. **What is the central theme of "New York Day Women?"**
   A. Love
   B. Hope
   C. Mother daughter relationships
   D. National Identity

7. **The following quote is an example of which literary element? "In Haiti when you get hit by a car, the owner of the car gets out and kicks you for getting blood on his bumper."**
    A. Setting
    B. Conflict
    C. Characterization
    D. Hyperbole

8. **How old is Suzette's mother?**
    A. 58
    B. 57
    C. 60
    D. 59

9. **Why doesn't Suzette's mother like taking the subway?**
    A. Because she doesn't understand how to navigate the subway
    B. Because she is afraid of being underground
    C. Because she is afraid of the strange people you meet when taking the subway
    D. Because she prefers to save money by walking

10. **What is the name of Caroline's fiancé?**
    A. Peter
    B. Edward
    C. Pele
    D. Eric

11. **How do Grace and Hermine calm Caroline down on the day of her wedding?**
    A. They give her a bath
    B. They feed her some bone soup
    C. They call Eric for her
    D. They buy her a prosthetic arm

12. **Where do Eric and Caroline get married?**
    A. In Eric's church
    B. At a courthouse
    C. At Mrs. Ruiz's house
    D. In Hermine's church

13. **What is Caroline missing?**
    A. Her right hand
    B. Her right forearm
    C. Her left hand
    D. Her left forearm

14. **Where is Caroline's fiancé from?**
    A. The Dominican Republic
    B. Cuba
    C. Brooklyn
    D. The Bahamas

15. **The main theme of "Caroline's Wedding" is:**
    A. Mother daughter relationships
    B. Love
    C. Hope
    D. National identity

16. **What is Grace's nickname?**
    A. Lean baby
    B. Misery baby
    C. Haiti baby
    D. Older sissy

17. **What does the following quote from Grace's father mean? "With patience, you can see the navel of an ant"**
    A. Take time to see the details in life
    B. Life can be found in the littlest things
    C. Patience is a virtue
    D. Don't' waste time on the insignificant

18. **Why does Mrs. Ruiz's son die?**
    A. Because he tries to illegally immigrant to America
    B. He gets caught working without a green card
    C. Because he tries to hijack a plane
    D. He contracts a disease

19. **Grace compares herself to everything EXCEPT:**
    A. Unclaimed property
    B. A divorcee
    C. An abandoned child
    D. An indentured servant

20. **What does the color pink symbolize?**
    A. Romance
    B. Adoration
    C. Love
    D. Happiness

21. **Hermine wants Eric to do all of the following EXCEPT:**
    A. Give her a dowry for Caroline's hand
    B. Kiss up to her and shower her with compliments
    C. Bring his own father to ask Hermine for her blessing
    D. Officially come and ask her for permission to marry Caroline

22. **Which one of these other Krik? Krak! characters is also mentioned in "Caroline's Wedding?"**
   A. Lili
   B. Jacqueline
   C. Célianne
   D. Josephine

23. **Who is the narrator of "Women Like Us"?**
   A. An unidentified character
   B. Edwidge Danticat
   C. Grace
   D. Caroline's daughter

24. **What is "Krik? Krak!" compared to in "Women Like Us?"**
   A. The feel of a piece of paper
   B. A pot bubbling
   C. A mother's cry
   D. The sound of writing

25. **What is the extended metaphor in "Women Like Us" about?**
   A. Writing
   B. Freedom
   C. The 999 women
   D. Cooking

Quiz 4 Answer Key

1. **(C)** Because she wants to leave her perspective of the world behind when she dies
2. **(B)** The way it began
3. **(D)** Salt
4. **(B)** "What has this world come to when the sun can no longer warm God's creatures?"
5. **(A)** A soda
6. **(C)** Mother daughter relationships
7. **(D)** Hyperbole
8. **(D)** 59
9. **(C)** Because she is afraid of the strange people you meet when taking the subway
10. **(D)** Eric
11. **(A)** They give her a bath
12. **(B)** At a courthouse
13. **(D)** Her left forearm
14. **(D)** The Bahamas
15. **(A)** Mother daughter relationships
16. **(B)** Misery baby
17. **(A)** Take time to see the details in life
18. **(C)** Because he tries to hijack a plane
19. **(C)** An abandoned child
20. **(A)** Romance
21. **(A)** Give her a dowry for Caroline's hand
22. **(C)** Célianne
23. **(B)** Edwidge Danticat
24. **(D)** The sound of writing
25. **(A)** Writing

Krik? Krak! Bibliography

Amber Stewart, author of ClassicNote. Completed on June 15, 2016, copyright held by GradeSaver.

Updated and revised by Aaron Suduiko June 20, 2016. Copyright held by GradeSaver.

Edwidge Danticat . Krik? Krak!. New York : Soho Press Inc., 1995.

ed. Martin Munro . Edwidge Danticat: A Reader's Guide. Charlottesville : University of Virginia Press, 2010.

Laurent Dubois . Haiti: The Aftershocks of History. New York City : Henry Holt and Company, LLC. , 2012.

Biography.com Editors. "Edwidge Danticat Biography." A&E Television Networks. May 1, 2016. <http://www.biography.com/people/edwidge-danticat>.

Maya Jaggi. "Island Memories ." The Guardian . November 20, 2004. May 1, 2016. <http://www.theguardian.com/books/2004/nov/20/featuresreviews.guardianreview9>.

Joanne Omang. "Krik? Krak! Review." Washington Post . May 14, 1995. May 1, 2016. <https://www.washingtonpost.com/archive/entertainment/books/1995/05/14/fiction/a38537f9-cdfd-4c77-ae08-e22677b8560a/>.

Palash Ghosh . "Parsley Massacre: The Massacre That Still Haunts Haitian-Dominican Relations." International Business Times . October 15, 2012. June 1, 2016. <http://www.ibtimes.com/parsley-massacre-genocide-still-haunts-haiti-dominican-relations-846773>.

Essay Ties Between Womanhood and Motherhood

by Anonymous

In *Krik? Krak!* Edwidge Danticat expands on the difficult role women must fulfill in a corrupted Haitian society. She portrays some of these requirements through the various transformations in the story, "The Missing Peace". With this important text, Danticat indicates that maturity and sexuality are not identical, and that personal development is bound up with learning to deal with loss and learning to put society, and one's own place in it, in perspective.

Emilie comes as a tourist to Ville Rose in search for her lost mother. Her search mainly acts, however, to confirm her mother's death, take a step into reality, and begin the process of grieving. She feels disconnected from her mother and doesn't want her to go as she tells Lamort, "'I see my mother sinking into a river, and she keeps calling my name"' (116). Emilie can't save her mother even though she's calling Emilie for help, and Emilie feels useless. In an attempt to reach her mother and try to save her, Emilie goes to the graveyard. Although she already knows the outcome, she can't fully accept it. That night, after painfully witnessing soldiers pulling a dead man on the ground, she knows that she can't physically reach her mother. Instead, Emilie works on her mother's quilt, which helps her internally with her mom, and she says, "'I lost my mother and all my other dreams"' (121). Although this saddens Emilie, as she knows that she will never find her mom, she also accepts her mother's death.

Lamort helps Emilie overcome her grief by acting as a temporary mother to her. When they first converse, Lamort repeats to Emilie some wise comments that her grandmother told Lamort earlier. In addition, Emilie feels an instant connection as she tells Lamort that she sounds like a journalist. Later, Emilie mentions that her mother was a journalist as well. This connection strengthens between them, and later Emilie asks Lamort to stay with her during the night. Lamort agrees, "'because I know you are afraid"' (121). Lamort knows Emilie feels scared of sleeping without her mother in her dreams, so she replaces Emilie's mother to help her with the transition of losing her mother.

Although Lamort transforms into a mother, she doesn't completely feel like one until she changes her name. Literally, Lamort means "the dead" in French. Her grandmother doesn't give Lamort her mother's name, Marie Magdalène, because she blames Lamort for the death. Lamort doesn't immensely care about her name because she thinks that her grandmother makes all the decisions. Once she acts as a mother to Emilie, and transitions her into accepting the death, she feels ready to live with that name. Thus, she approaches her grandmother after returning home, "'I want you to call me by Marie Magdalène.' I liked the sound of that" (122). She's happy with her name and feels more connected to her mother as well. Her grandmother looks “pained” to call Lamort by her precious daughter’s name, yet she also knows that she must let go and satisfy Lamort (122). In this way, Lamort helps her grandmother, similarly to Emilie, with accepting her daughter’s death.

Lamort changes her name and acts like a mother mainly because she truly transforms into a woman. In the beginning of the story, Raymond tells Lamort, “‘I know I can make you feel like a woman’” (103). He, like other men in the book, wrongly believes that a girl becomes a woman when she has sex. He pressures Lamort further and asks, “’so why don’t you let me?’” (103). He still doesn’t understand how a girl truly becomes a woman. Instead, he tries to persuade her to have sex with him because he knows that she wants to feel like a woman. Furthermore, her grandmother says to Lamort, “‘See, you can be a pretty girl” (108). The grandmother hints that Lamort wasn’t pretty before, and she also stresses the fact that Lamort’s a girl. The American tourist is the only person who views Lamort as mature, helpful, and motherly. Emilie explains to her, “‘They say a girl becomes a woman when she loses her mother,’ she said. ‘You, child, were born a woman’” (116). Emilie lives in America, where girls who are Lamort’s age don’t act like a woman. She’s pleasantly surprised and acknowledges that Lamort is young, and yet, she still acts like a woman.

Similarly to Lamort, Emilie transforms into a woman through acceptance and motherhood. Although Emilie loses her mother, she doesn’t accept it at first, and thus withholds from becoming a women. Like a child, she also relies on Lamort to comfort and protect her in the night. In addition, she sews a quilt that her mother left unfinished. Through this process, she connects with her mother and replaces her, just like Lamort adopts her mother’s name. Furthermore, Emilie cares for Lamort like a mother and explains, “‘I didn’t get in a fight with them because I did not want them to hurt you’” (121). She purposefully protected Lamort instead of choosing her natural instinct to fight. Once Emilie begins to act motherly, accepts her mother’s death, and connects with her mother, she realizes, “‘I became a woman last night’” (121).

During all these personal transformations, the town’s moral changes as well. In the beginning of the story, Raymond tells Lamort to never forget the password when she’s in trouble. The password essentially serves as a common goal or moral: “peace”. This peace has no effect on Toto when he confronts Lamort and Emilie outside the graveyard. And Raymond explains to Lamort, “‘The password has changed,’ he said. ‘Stop saying ‘peace’’” (119). The password that served as the main goal and holding everyone together turns nonexistent. There is no peace. Despite the missing peace around them, Lamort and Emilie feel calm inside. They are women, and don’t act anxious during hectic times.

Emilie and Lamort transform in different ways to ultimately become women. Because they both lost their mothers, they find unity and strength. They help each other in the process of becoming women. Both act motherly, overcome their immature weaknesses, and take on the role of their own mothers. They realize that becoming a woman is difficult and painful. Acting as a woman requires many responsibilities as well, including keeping posterity. The grandmother points out that keeping posterity is how a woman lives her life. Emilie wants to learn more about her mother for posterity. Yet, she doesn't find any posterity except for herself. She realizes that she will have posterity from just living her life as a woman.

The ideas of becoming and acting as a woman from "The Missing Peace" echo throughout the whole book. Raymond, like other Haitian men, tried to turn Lamort into a woman by having sex. However, performing sex does not make a woman. Women comfort others in a time of need, live independently, and care for their children. Even if the world and their surroundings are violent, frightening, and chaotic, women remain peaceful and constant. Above all, they form an inseparable bond that can never be broken. They are the strength, peace, and comfort when all else fails.

ClassicNotes

GradeSaver™

Getting you the grade since 1999™

Other ClassicNotes from GradeSaver™

ClassicNotes

Getting you the grade since 1999™

Other ClassicNotes from GradeSaver™

- Mother Courage and Her Children
- Mrs. Dalloway
- Mrs. Warren's Profession
- Much Ado About Nothing
- Murder in the Cathedral
- My Antonia
- My Brilliant Friend
- My Children! My Africa!
- Mythology
- Narrative of the Life of Frederick Douglass
- Native Son
- Nervous Conditions
- Never Let Me Go
- New Introductory Lectures on Psychoanalysis
- News from Nowhere
- Nickel and Dimed: On (Not) Getting By in America
- Night
- Nine Stories
- Njal's Saga
- No Exit
- No Longer at Ease
- North and South
- Northanger Abbey
- North by Northwest
- Norwegian Wood
- Notes from Underground
- Notorious
- Number the Stars
- Oedipus Rex or Oedipus the King
- Of Mice and Men
- Of Modern Poetry
- Oliver Twist
- On Beauty
- One Day in the Life of Ivan Denisovich
- One Flew Over the Cuckoo's Nest
- One Flew Over the Cuckoo's Nest (Film)
- One Hundred Years of Solitude
- On Liberty
- On the Road
- On the Waterfront
- O Pioneers
- Orlando
- Oroonoko
- Oryx and Crake
- Othello
- Our Town
- Outcasts United
- Outliers
- Pale Fire

For our full list of over 250 Study Guides, Quizzes, Sample College Application Essays, Literature Essays and E-texts, visit:

www.gradesaver.com

ClassicNotes

GradeSaver™

Getting you the grade since 1999™

Other ClassicNotes from GradeSaver™

Pamela: Or Virtue Rewarded
Paper Towns
Parable of the Sower
Paradise
Paradise Lost
Passing
Paul Revere's Ride
Peace Like a River
Pedro Paramo
Percy Shelley: Poems
Perfume: The Story of a Murderer
Persepolis: The Story of a Childhood
Persuasion
Phaedra
Phaedrus
Pilgrim's Progress
Poems of W.B. Yeats: The Rose
Poems of W.B. Yeats: The Tower
Poe's Poetry
Poe's Short Stories
Poetry
Politics and the English Language
Pope's Poems and Prose
Portrait of the Artist as a Young Man
Pretty Woman
Pride and Prejudice
Private Memoirs and Confessions of a Justified Sinner
Prometheus Bound
Psycho
Pudd'nhead Wilson
Purple Hibiscus
Pygmalion
Rabbit, Run
Rashomon
Ray Bradbury: Short Stories
Reached
Reading Lolita in Tehran
Rear Window
Rebecca
Reflections on Gandhi
Regeneration
Return of the Native
Rhinoceros
Richard II
Richard III
Riders to the Sea
Rip Van Winkle and Other Stories
Robert Browning: Poems
Robert Frost: Poems
Robinson Crusoe
Roll of Thunder, Hear My Cry

For our full list of over 250 Study Guides, Quizzes, Sample College Application Essays, Literature Essays and E-texts, visit:

www.gradesaver.com

ClassicNotes

Getting you the grade since 1999™

Other ClassicNotes from GradeSaver™

The Hound of the Baskervilles
The House of Bernarda Alba
The House of the Seven Gables
The House of the Spirits
The Hunger Games
The Iceman Cometh
The Idea of Order at Key West
The Importance of Being Earnest
The Infinite Sea
The Interlopers
Their Eyes Were Watching God
The Island of Dr. Moreau
The Jew of Malta
The Joy Luck Club
The Jungle
The Kill Order
The Kite Runner
The Lais of Marie de France
The Legend of Sleepy Hollow
The Library of Babel
The Life of Olaudah Equiano
The Lightning Thief
The Lion and the Jewel
The Lion, the Witch and the Wardrobe
The Lone Ranger and Tonto Fistfight in Heaven
The Lord of the Rings: The Fellowship of the Ring
The Lord of the Rings: The Return of the King
The Lord of the Rings: The Two Towers
The Lottery and Other Stories
The Lovely Bones
The Love Song of J. Alfred Prufrock
The Magician's Nephew
The Maltese Falcon (1941 Film)
The Man in the High Castle
The Man of Mode
The Marrow of Tradition
The Master and Margarita

For our full list of over 250 Study Guides, Quizzes,
Sample College Application Essays, Literature Essays and E-texts, visit:

www.gradesaver.com

ClassicNotes

Getting you the grade since 1999™

Other ClassicNotes from GradeSaver™

To Kill a Mockingbird
Top Girls
To the Lighthouse
Touching Spirit Bear
Trainspotting (Film)
Treasure Island
Trifles
Troilus and Cressida
Tropic of Cancer
Tropic of Capricorn
Tuesdays With Morrie
Twelfth Night
Twilight
Ulysses
Un Chien Andalou
Uncle Tom's Cabin
Uncle Vanya
Under the Feet of Jesus
Untouchable
Up From Slavery
Ursula Le Guin: Short Stories
Utilitarianism
Utopia
Vanity Fair
Vanka
Villette
Volpone
Waiting for Godot
Waiting for Lefty
Waiting for the Barbarians
Walden
Walled States, Waning Sovereignty
Walt Whitman: Poems
War and Peace
Washington Square
We
Weep Not, Child
We Need New Names
What is the What
W. H. Auden: Poems
Where Are You Going, Where Have You Been?
Where the Red Fern Grows
White Fang
White Noise
White Teeth
Who's Afraid of Virginia Woolf
Wide Sargasso Sea
Wieland
Wilfred Owen: Poems
Winesburg, Ohio
Wise Blood
Women in Love
Wonder

For our full list of over 250 Study Guides, Quizzes, Sample College Application Essays, Literature Essays and E-texts, visit:

www.gradesaver.com

ClassicNotes

Getting you the grade since 1999™

Other ClassicNotes from GradeSaver™

Wordsworth's Poetical Works
Woyzeck
Wuthering Heights
Year of Wonders
Yonnondio: From the Thirties
Young Goodman Brown and Other
Hawthorne Short Stories
Zeitoun
Z For Zachariah

Made in United States
Orlando, FL
07 September 2022

22122815R00075